MODEL RAILROAD HANDBOOK NO. 3

BY LINN H. WESTCOTT

PLANS

OTHER FEATURES

KALMBACH BOOKS

First printing, 1956. Second printing, 1957. Third printing, 1961. Fourth printing, 1963. Fifth printing, 1967. Sixth printing, 1969. Seventh printing, 1970. Eighth printing, 1972. Ninth printing, 1974. Tenth printing, 1975. Eleventh printing, 1976. Twelfth printing, 1978. Thirteenth printing, 1980. Fourteenth printing, 1982. Fifteenth printing, 1984. Sixteenth printing, 1987. Seventeenth printing, 1988. Eighteenth printing, 1989. Nineteenth printing, 1992.

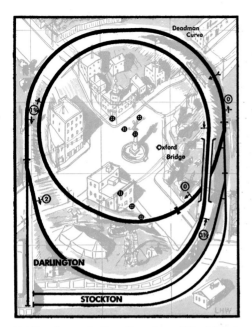

1. Stockton & Darlington RR. Very sharp curves

Even a very small railroad can have a yard by folding it around the outside of the oval. Streets are built at an angle deliberately to get the effect of more space. Keep buildings small but with plenty of detail.

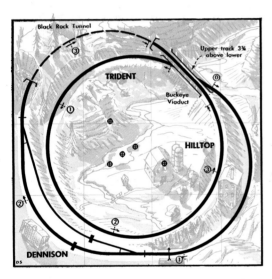

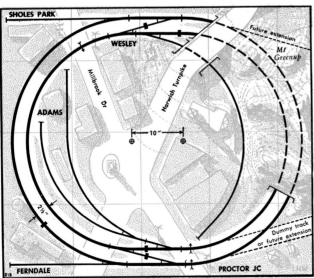

What scale do you build?

N SCALE

The plans in this book were prepared before N scale was developed. However, you can reduce any plan to suit N scale needs by following the dimensions given in the tables. Remember, though, that any aisleways running into the table space must be maintained wide enough for you to walk conveniently. You have great freedom in planning with N scale. The ruled lines on all plans are 6″ apart.

TT SCALE

You're lucky, because no matter what the size of your railroad room, you have a wide choice of plans that will fit it. The ruled lines across all plans are 9″ apart for you. Such dimensions as elevations, turntable diameters and special radii (but not angles) should be multiplied by ¾″ to get the correct figure for your use. Read the text and you'll find other suggestions that will help you.

HO SCALE

The ruled lines across all plans are 1 foot apart. Other dimensions such as radii, elevations, etc., are shown in inches for your use. Many of these railroads were originally built in the HO size. Be sure to read the text for other ideas and helpful kinks.

S SCALE

Your scale is a good compromise between space and construction detail, and many of these plans take advantage of both. The ruled lines across all plans are spaced 18″ apart for your use. Add half again to the printed dimensions shown for elevations, radii, turntables, etc., to obtain your correct size. Angles remain unchanged. On some large plans you may want to cut an extra opening or two through the scenery so you won't have to reach too far from the edge of a table to reach critical switchwork. Read the text for more suggestions in layout and scenic construction.

O SCALE

The ruled lines across all plans are spaced 2 feet apart for your use. Elevations, turntable diameters, special radii and other figured dimensions on the plans should be doubled for your use. Angles remain unchanged. Many of these plans were originally built in O gauge, but in some you'll find that the reach from the edge of the table to critical trackwork may be a little far. The remedy is the same as we suggested for S gaugers: cut a small access hatch through the scenery.

Railroads for very small tables

See page 70 for more data.

2. Kettle Hills & Eastern RR. Very sharp curves

Two-level operation is one way to get the effect of a larger railroad into a small space.

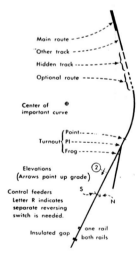

3. Bay State Western Ry. (At left.) Sharp curves

A double-track railroad needs at least one crossover, preferably two. To save space, one switch of each crossover is flopped from the usual position so that it can extend into the curve. This is always a good trick in track planning.

4. Reddy River & Piedras RR. (Opposite page.) Sharp curves

This railroad can handle two trains, or you can switch one while another runs. Originally this was just a sketch in MODEL RAILROADER magazine but it has so many good points that we've figured it more carefully for your use.

How to choose your track plan

THE first step in choosing a plan in this book is to discard all the layouts that are too big for the space you have. The plans are arranged, for the most part, in groups of gradually increasing size; you can find all sizes compared in the index on page 70. Later on I'll show you how plans can be adjusted to the exact size and shape of your table or room. After you have narrowed the selection to those plans which will fit your space, the choice depends on what you like.

While searching through the book for plans, turn the pages upside down, then to the right or left. Look at all the plans in a mirror, too. In this way you won't overlook any plan that's well suited to your space.

What plan would I choose if I wanted a good average layout?

Look for a plan with one- or two-lap main lines. If space allows, these should have return loops in each direction so trains can be turned to go clockwise or counterclockwise for more variety of operation. An average layout should have some space for scenery, but if the area is small, getting in enough track is usually more of a problem.

Selected one-lap and two-lap ovals:
1, 3, 4, 16, 18, 19, 20, 22, 23, 25, 29, 36, 38, 46, 54, 60, 74, 79.
Selected plans with one return track:
13, 27, 42, 50, 61.
Selected plans with two return tracks:
24, 53, 54, 57, 58, 59, 65, 77, 84, 100.

What kind of plan is best for switching?

It doesn't matter much how the main line goes as long as you have yards and industrial spurs in good supply. Take any plan in this book and add more spurs and yards if there aren't already enough. If you prefer way-freight operation, pick a plan with a long main line with spurs frequently turning off in every direction. If you prefer yard switching, keep the main line more simple and choose a plan that allows for many yard tracks.

Railroads featuring switching:
3, 4, 6, 7, 8, **9**, 10, 11, 12, 18, **20**, **23**, 24, 25, **26**, **27**, 33, and most plans from 38 onward. Bold face indicates plans where switching in the yard doesn't have to interfere with mainline running.

What plans are best for railroadlike train operation?

The essence of railroad train operation is to make up a train in the yard and then send it over the main line (or perhaps a branch) to another yard or terminal. This is called point-to-point operation by model railroaders, but you don't necessarily require a point-to-point plan to accomplish it. Any plan with a main line of some length can be used if the terminals are arranged well. You can connect two terminals into any oval so that a train must use most of the oval main line when going from one terminal to the other, like this:

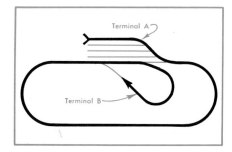

By using a loop for one terminal, you'll usually have more space to build a bigger yard at the main terminal. Notice how this was done in plan 100. The wye allows trains to enter the two-lap oval going either way. After passing the wye, a train is forced to stay on the main line all the way around. There are no short cuts as they wouldn't improve operation.

The train reaches a terminal only after completely circuiting the main line. In this plan the train has a choice of terminals: it can go back into the original yard (as though it had reached a different city), or it can terminate in one of the return loops — Little Miami Loop or Barberton Cut-off. From these it is immediately ready to make another trip over the main line in the opposite direction.

The point is that it's nice to have an oval type of plan for test and display runs, but an oval can also be arranged for railroadlike point-to-point operation as well. For most men a plan that combines both kinds of operation is more satisfying.

Pure point-to-point plans have a simplicity and charm of their own, especially if track never doubles back on itself. I think you'll see this better than I can explain in words if you look over several point-to-point plans.

Point-to-point railroads:
5, 8, 10, **40**, **43**, 44, 45, 47, 51, 55, 68, **69**, 72, 73, 75, 78, 81, 83, 87, **94**, **95**, **96**, 101. Bold numbers are loop-to-loop plans.
Railroads suited to both point-to-point and oval-type running:
9, 17, 18, 24, 26, 27, 28, 34, 35, 42, 48, 50, 53, 54, 59, 61, 62, 63, 65, 66, 67, 70, 72, 73, 77, 82, 84, 86, 88, 89, 90, 92, 93, 97, 98, 99, 100. Plans 64 and 76 are out-and-back type.

What kind of plans are most suited to running two or more trains at once?

On most plans, you can run one train on the main line while another is switched in the yards. Sometimes provision can be made so the two never interfere.

A two-track main line is obviously suited to running two or more trains. Put one on each track and just let

(Continued on next page)

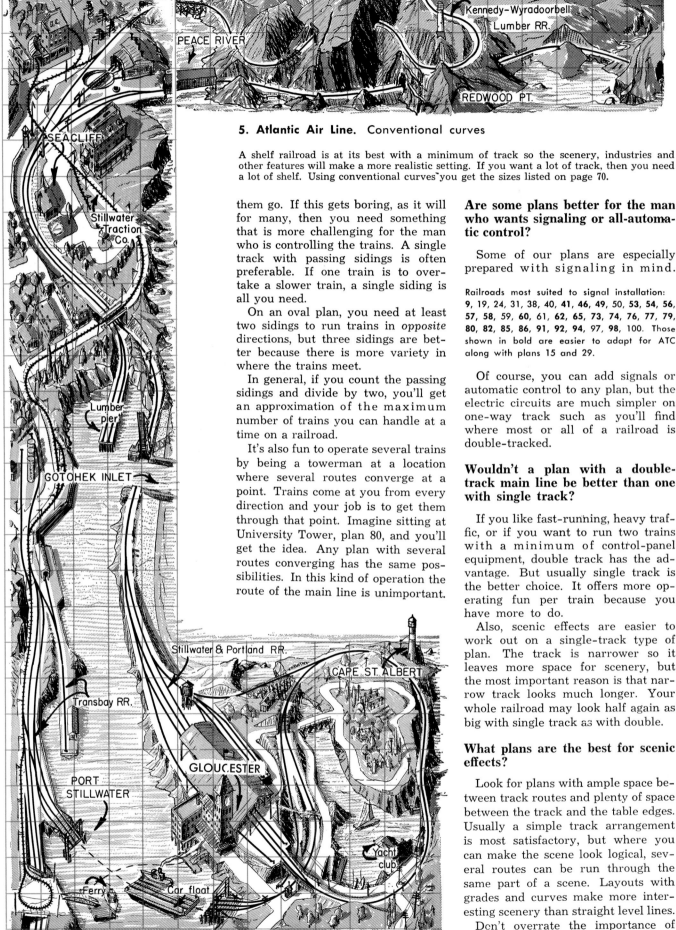

PEACE RIVER

Kennedy-Wyradoorbell
Lumber RR.

REDWOOD PT.

SEACLIFF

Stillwater
Traction
Co.

Lumber
pier

GOTCHEK INLET

Stillwater & Portland RR.

CAPE ST. ALBERT

Transbay RR.

GLOUCESTER

PORT
STILLWATER

Yacht
club

Ferry   Car float

5. Atlantic Air Line. Conventional curves

A shelf railroad is at its best with a minimum of track so the scenery, industries and other features will make a more realistic setting. If you want a lot of track, then you need a lot of shelf. Using conventional curves you get the sizes listed on page 70.

them go. If this gets boring, as it will for many, then you need something that is more challenging for the man who is controlling the trains. A single track with passing sidings is often preferable. If one train is to overtake a slower train, a single siding is all you need.

On an oval plan, you need at least two sidings to run trains in *opposite* directions, but three sidings are better because there is more variety in where the trains meet.

In general, if you count the passing sidings and divide by two, you'll get an approximation of the maximum number of trains you can handle at a time on a railroad.

It's also fun to operate several trains by being a towerman at a location where several routes converge at a point. Trains come at you from every direction and your job is to get them through that point. Imagine sitting at University Tower, plan 80, and you'll get the idea. Any plan with several routes converging has the same possibilities. In this kind of operation the route of the main line is unimportant.

Are some plans better for the man who wants signaling or all-automatic control?

Some of our plans are especially prepared with signaling in mind.

Railroads most suited to signal installation: 9, 19, 24, 31, 38, 40, 41, 46, 49, 50, 53, 54, 56, 57, 58, 59, 60, 61, 62, 65, 73, 74, 76, 77, 79, 80, 82, 85, 86, 91, 92, 94, 97, 98, 100. Those shown in bold are easier to adapt for ATC along with plans 15 and 29.

Of course, you can add signals or automatic control to any plan, but the electric circuits are much simpler on one-way track such as you'll find where most or all of a railroad is double-tracked.

Wouldn't a plan with a double-track main line be better than one with single track?

If you like fast-running, heavy traffic, or if you want to run two trains with a minimum of control-panel equipment, double track has the advantage. But usually single track is the better choice. It offers more operating fun per train because you have more to do.

Also, scenic effects are easier to work out on a single-track type of plan. The track is narrower so it leaves more space for scenery, but the most important reason is that narrow track looks much longer. Your whole railroad may look half again as big with single track as with double.

What plans are the best for scenic effects?

Look for plans with ample space between track routes and plenty of space between the track and the table edges. Usually a simple track arrangement is most satisfactory, but where you can make the scene look logical, several routes can be run through the same part of a scene. Layouts with grades and curves make more interesting scenery than straight level lines.

Don't overrate the importance of scenery in choosing a plan. You can

Continued on page 19

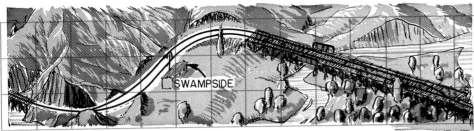

How to build your railroad from plans

IN BOOKS about model railroad carpentry, track laying, and scenery construction, you'll find that you have a choice between "flat top" and "grid" (open top) types of table construction. In a nutshell, the type of table with a flat plywood sheet for a top saves a little time in construction providing you build a one-level type of railroad. The open or grid type of construction is better for scenic reasons, but may take a little longer to build. On a multilevel railroad, grid construction undoubtedly saves time.

All plans can be built by grid methods.

How do I transfer track locations from the printed plans to the railroad framework?

Our plans have lines ruled across them each way in uniform spacing. The spacing represents:

      6″ for N scale construction.
      9″ for TT scale construction.
      12″ for HO scale construction.
      18″ for S scale construction.
      24″ for O scale construction.

If you draw these same lines across the top of your framework or plywood surface, you can estimate how many inches any feature is from the nearest lines and transfer this location from the plan to the corresponding lines on the railroad table. For greater accuracy, measure the scale inches from the nearest lines on the plan.

We've printed scales on the margins of our index pages for your convenience. Many of the plans are drawn in ¾″, ⅜″, or ³⁄₁₆″ scale. You'll find an ordinary ruler has the desired six or 12 marks per square on the plan for measuring anything that falls between lines.

Isn't it a good idea to work from large plans?

Large plans are better if you plan to make changes of your own. But otherwise you should get along fine with plans just as they come in this book. This is because so few dimensions on a track plan are really critical. We don't ordinarily permit persons to copy plans from our publications without written consent. However, you have our permission to get an enlarged copy made of any plan if it is for building your own personal home railroad. Photocopy firms in the nearest city are well equipped to do this for two or three dollars.

It's also easy to enlarge plans by drawing lines 1½″, 2″, or 3″ apart each way on a piece of paper. Then you copy the location of track one square at a time, enlarging it by hand from the squares on the plans in the book. This may sound tedious, but it isn't as bad as you might expect. Usually freehand work will be accurate enough, but double check the locations of curve centers and switch ladders for safety.

What parts of the track should be located carefully?

The curves near the corners of a table often have a critical location. Ladder tracks in yards should also be arranged accurately or else there may not be enough room for all the switches. Where tracks are closely parallel, be sure tracks are separated enough so cars on one track won't sideswipe engines or cars on the other. Here are the minimum distances to maintain between track centers for various curves:

	Sharp curves	Conventional curves	Broad curves
N	1¼″	1⅛″	1″
TT	1⅞″	1¹¹⁄₁₆″	1½″
HO	2½″	2¼″	2″
S	3¾″	3⅜″	3″
O	5″	4½″	4″

Straight tracks can be as close as 13 scale feet from center to center, and this looks very realistic. However, our plans and most builders use the separation shown above for broad curves for straight track as well.

We used this same distance as the clearance from track to edge of table or wall in most of our plans. If you have difficulty making things fit, you can cut this in half. You might encounter such a difficulty if the switches you use are longer than NMRA size, as they frequently are. More about this later.

Can I use sectional track to build from these plans?

Yes, but you'll have to cut many short pieces of straight and curved

Continued on page 7

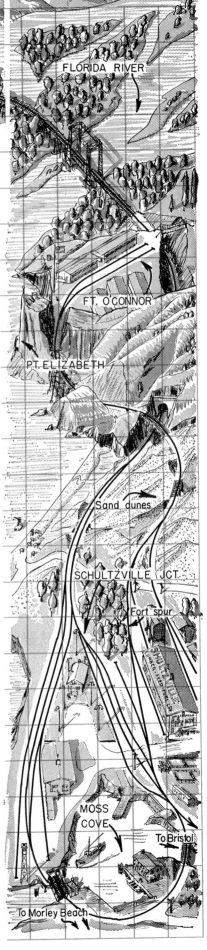

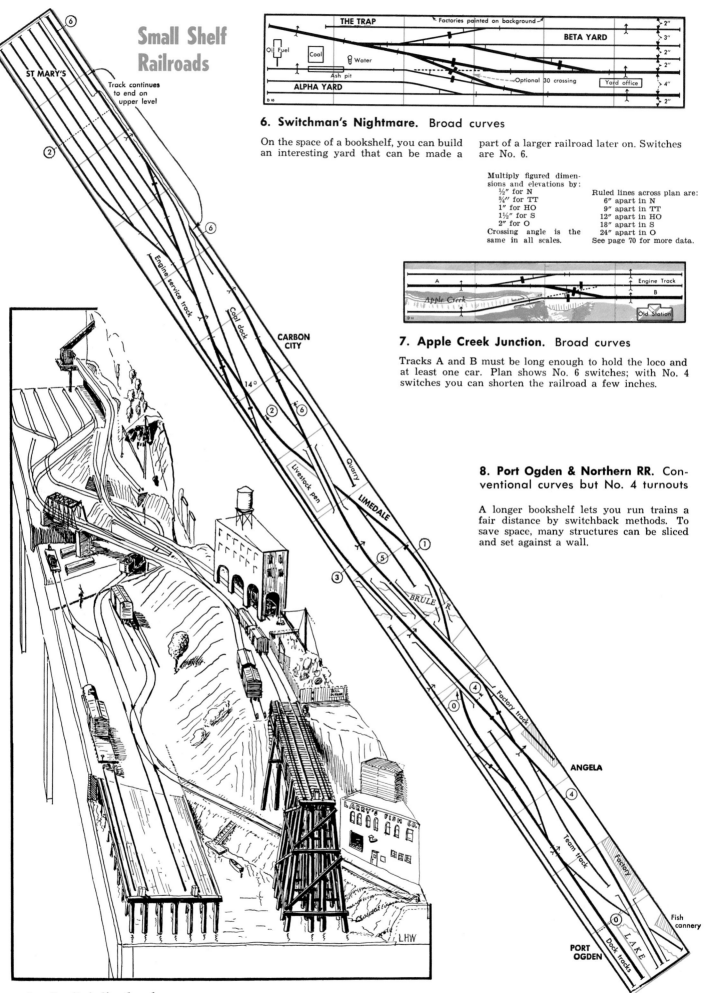

Small Shelf Railroads

ST MARY'S

Track continues to end on upper level

Engine service track

Coal dock

14°

CARBON CITY

Livestock pen

Quarry

LIMEDALE

BRULE R.

Factory track

Team Track

Factory

ANGELA

Fish cannery

PORT OGDEN

Dock tracks

LAKE

LHW

THE TRAP

Factories painted on background

BETA YARD

Oil Fuel

Coal

Water

Ash pit

ALPHA YARD

Optional 30 crossing

Yard office

2"
3"
2"
2"
4"
2"

D.10

6. Switchman's Nightmare. Broad curves

On the space of a bookshelf, you can build an interesting yard that can be made a part of a larger railroad later on. Switches are No. 6.

Multiply figured dimensions and elevations by:
½" for N
¾" for TT
1" for HO
1½" for S
2" for O
Crossing angle is the same in all scales.

Ruled lines across plan are:
6" apart in N
9" apart in TT
12" apart in HO
18" apart in S
24" apart in O
See page 70 for more data.

A

Apple Creek

Engine Track

B

Old Station

D.11

7. Apple Creek Junction. Broad curves

Tracks A and B must be long enough to hold the loco and at least one car. Plan shows No. 6 switches; with No. 4 switches you can shorten the railroad a few inches.

8. Port Ogden & Northern RR. Conventional curves but No. 4 turnouts

A longer bookshelf lets you run trains a fair distance by switchback methods. To save space, many structures can be sliced and set against a wall.

LARRY'S FISH CO.

Continued from page 5

track because only rarely will a plan have track that matches an even number of pieces of sectional track.

If you have a little more space than needed, you won't need as many short sections of track. You can paraphrase the plan, build the same track arrangement but let the dimensions yield to the units of the track sections.

Is there any particular order for locating track lines on the tables?

Definitely yes. Unless you have lots of extra space, it would be asking for trouble to start locating track at the yard and work around the main line to the other end of the railroad. You'll avoid a good many pitfalls if you work this way instead:

1. Locate all curves that swing near the outer corners of your space. You can make a cardboard template to the correct radius and use it like a curved ruler. (Another way is to use a string or wooden boom and swing a pencil from the curve center.) Draw the curve beyond each end for a ways.

2. Locate other curves in the same way. Don't worry about straight tracks between curves yet.

3. Locate the main and ladder tracks of your yard. Sometimes they're the same track.

4. Add connecting tracks everywhere. Usually these will be straight, but often you can get a beautiful effect by using a gradual curve with little or no straight track *even in places where the plans show straight track*. Plan 49 has these sweeping curves in place of straight track. Plan 50 also has a few.

5. Where connecting tracks include track switches, locate the straight track first. Then locate the branch as a straight line at the proper angle. The angle is 1″ in 4″ for a No. 4 switch (14¼ degrees) or 1″ in 6″ for a No. 6 switch (9½ degrees).

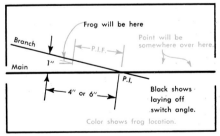

6. Wherever these lines cross is called the P.I. (point of intersection) of the switch, and using the P.I. is the best way to locate a switch. From the P.I. you mark off a distance obtained by multiplying the switch number by the gauge to find the place where the frog of the switch will come. Do not use the point end of a switch for measurements as it varies with different manufacturers.

Here are the P.I.-to-frog distances for switch location figured for you:

Scale	P.I.F. for No. 4	P.I.F. for No. 6
N	1⁵⁄₁₆″	1³¹⁄₃₂″
TT	1⅞″	2¹³⁄₁₆″
HO	2⅝″	3¹⁵⁄₁₆″
S	3½″	5¼″
O	5″	7½″

Our plans show marks for the switch frog and point with fine crossties. However, it is better to use the P.I.F. method for locating switches than to measure them off from plans; fewer errors will occur and those you do make will tend to be self-compensating.

How do I use the printed dimensions, say for O gauge? Other gauges?

Track elevations, minimum radii and other dimensions, are printed directly on our plans and captions. Multiply these figures by:
  ½″ for N scale railroads.
  ¾″ for TT scale railroads.
  1″ for HO scale railroads.
  1½″ for S scale railroads.
  2″ for O scale railroads.
Do not multiply angles as they are the same in all scales. Switch sizes are also angles, so they're the same in every scale too.

What size are the switches on the plans?

Except where noted, No. 4 switches are used with sharp curves, No. 6 with all others. Very sharp curves marked 15″ or 16″ radius can be used with No. 4 turnouts as well, but usually special switches or stub switches that have a curve right through the entire switch are used. You usually have to build these yourself.

What is a stub switch? It's like an ordinary switch at the frog end except that there may be a curve through the frog. However, at the point end the approach rails are swung from one branch to the other like the end of a turntable. Stub switches were common on railroads years ago and are still found on old track. Their advantage is that they allow a sharp curve to run right through the switch gracefully, and they have an "old-time" look.

What if I can't get as many switches into the space as you show on the plan?

This can happen, especially at the throat of a yard or between several crossovers. We used NMRA (National Model Railroad Association) switch dimensions for our plans. But commercially made switches are sometimes made extra long. The distance from point to frog is not only too long, but there also may be an inch or more of straight track in front of the points.

In most places you won't notice this, but if switchwork is tight, feel perfectly safe in either bending the point end of a switch into the adjoining curve or in actually shortening the switch and even the switch points. The length from point to frog can be as little as 1½ times the P.I.F. listed in the last answer.

What are the curve radii used in the plans?

Plans are classed with sharp, conventional, or broad curves in the index on page 70. Here are the minimum radii we used for each class:

Scale	Sharp	Conventional	Broad
N	9″	12″	15″
TT	13½″	18″	22½″
HO	18″	24″	30″
S	27″	36″	45″
O	36″	48″	60″
Turnout size:	4	6	6

Where there's a second track around the curve it will either have a different center or else the following radius is used from the same center.

Scale	Sharp	Conventional	Broad
N	10¼″	13⅛″	16″
TT	15⅜″	19¹¹⁄₁₆″	24″
HO	20½″	26¼″	32″
S	30¾″	39⅜″	48″
O	41″	52½″	64″

How can I follow your recommendations for radii of 26¼″ in HO, etc., when track is made in 26″ radius instead?

Engines and cars will sideswipe when only 2″ separation is used in HO between curves of 24″ and 26″ radii. The problem is similar in O gauge, S, TT, and N. Even the 2¼″ separation we recommend for HO isn't enough for some articulateds and other long engines.

The answer is to spring the commercial radius track out enough so it follows the slightly wider recommended radius line. Notice that the second track paralleling an 18″ radius track in our plans is given as 20½″, while commercial track comes in 20″ or 21″ instead. Here, if you cannot spring the 20″ track, you can add ½″ of straight track at each end of a 90° curve; 1″ in the end of an oval, etc.

How do I use the track elevations shown on the plans?

First, multiply all the elevations shown to convert them to your scale. If you work in N, multiply by ½″; in TT, by ¾″. In HO the elevations are already correct. In S, add half again; and in O, double the elevations.

Now locate the part of the plan showing zero elevation at any chosen height from the floor or table top. Use a carpenter's level to transfer this zero to other parts of the railroad, then add the elevations you calculated for any point.

Between the places where we've

Continued on next page

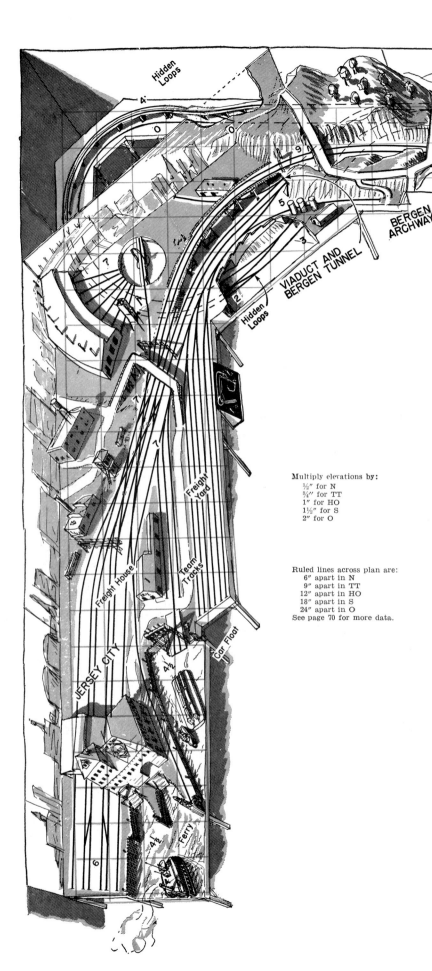

Multiply elevations by:
½″ for N
¾″ for TT
1″ for HO
1½″ for S
2″ for O

Ruled lines across plan are:
6″ apart in N
9″ apart in TT
12″ apart in HO
18″ apart in S
24″ apart in O
See page 70 for more data.

Continued from page 7

shown elevations, keep the grade ris-
ing or falling evenly. At the places
where we've shown elevation figures,
the grade usually changes. It may be
to a steeper grade or it may be a summit or sag. In any case, bend the
change of grade gradually over a car
length or more of distance. We've
tried to arrange elevations so you
won't have to have any of these "ver-
tical curves" running through a track
switch.

Small arrows next to the elevation
dots always point upgrade. If the
point is a summit, the arrowhead just
touches the dotted line, rather than
crossing it. At the foot of a grade,
the other end of the arrow touches
the dots.

Is there plenty of clearance for building bridges?

We've used a separation of 29 scale
feet from base of rail to base of rail
as the separation of one track above
another. This is 2″ in N, 3″ in TT, 4″
in HO, 6″ in S, and 8″ in O.

This should give you enough clearance to build a roadway with plenty of
room above the lower track. Later
you can saw out the roadway and
build the bridge.

In a few places, tighter clearances
(less than 4″ in HO) are indicated on
the plan. In these tight places you'll
need thinner support for the upper
track. The clearance from lower rail
top to the underside of a bridge must
be at least:

1½″ in N scale.
2⅛″ in TT scale.
3″ in HO scale.
4⅛″ in S scale.
5½″ in O scale.

Must I cut gaps in the rails exactly where you show them?

You can cut them anywhere within
half a car length or so of where we
show gaps, and it doesn't matter
whether gaps are opposite or stag-
gered. To move a gap farther might

Continued on page 67

GUYMARD UNDERPASS

Pusher Siding

GRAHAM JCT.

Gulf Summit

STARRUCCA VIADUCT

Built over depressed benchwork

LANESBORO

MILL RIFT

Canal Bridge

DELAWARE RIVER

D&H CANAL LOCKS

MILL RIFT BRIDGE

Cable Ferry

L. H. WESTCOTT AUG. 18 1955

9. Erie RR.

Like many of the smaller plans in this book, this railroad has many details patterned after features on a real railroad. Most of the buildings, for instance, are fashioned from photos of real buildings along the Erie. Track arrangements at Jersey City, Guymard and Starrucca are also similar to the prototype. If you model in this way from a railroad you are familiar with, it will add to the fun both for you and those who look at your work.

How to change plans to suit your needs

WHEN your railroad space isn't the same size and shape as the plan you like, you can still adjust the plan to make the best use of the space. You may want to change a plan for other reasons too, such as to borrow the yard from one plan for use in another.

Even if you're not sure you need changes, it's good to think about them. Think about each suggestion we make with respect to your own plan, and listen to comments of friends, too. One change that sometimes helps is to make the high tracks low and the low tracks high, a sort of inverting. (You can do this safely by subtracting each elevation on a plan from the highest elevation shown.) This trick can put a troublesome track under the yard instead of over it, or it may raise some part of the railroad to clear a pump or some other obstruction in your basement.

The yards and terminals in our plans are usually located where they can make the most use of the space, or else where we thought you could get at them easily for operating. But if a wall or some other feature makes

Continued on page 38

Small railroads

All plans to same scale.

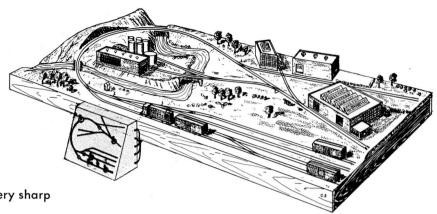

10. Pittsburgh, Midvale & Ironton RR. Very sharp curve

Doubling back the main line gives the effect of a train going somewhere after it completes its yard switching. To build this in the space shown, a 15" radius curve must be used. This kind of plan is easy to combine into a bigger railroad you might build someday.

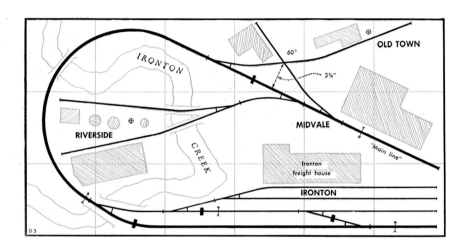

Ruled lines across plan are:
6" apart in N
9" apart in TT
12" apart in HO
18" apart in S
24" apart in O
See page 70 for more data.

11. Logan Street Yard. Conventional curves

You can operate this small corner-type yard just as it is, but if you have a longer space, extend the track to the left. You can put a lot of superdetail into a plan like this. The conventional curves will handle any loco.

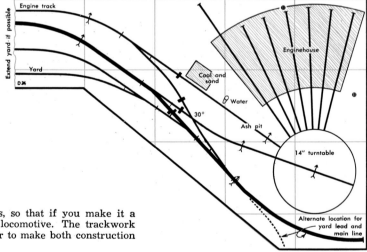

12. Mechanic Street Yard. Conventional curves

This yard also uses conventional curves and No. 6 switches, so that if you make it a part of a large layout later, you can handle any length of locomotive. The trackwork is made particularly complicated for so small a yard in order to make both construction and operation more interesting.

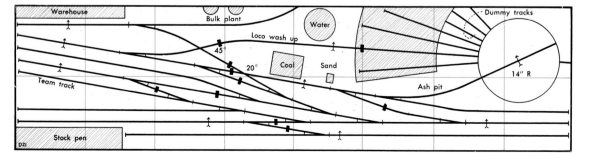

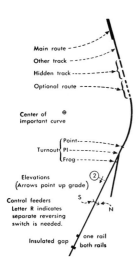

Main route -----
Other track -----
Hidden track -----
Optional route -----

Center of ⊕
important curve

Turnout {Point -----
Pl -----
Frog -----

Elevations ②
(Arrows point up grade)

Control feeders   S
Letter R indicates   N
separate reversing
switch is needed.

Insulated gap   one rail
both rails

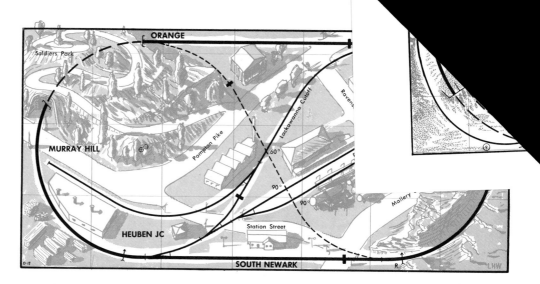

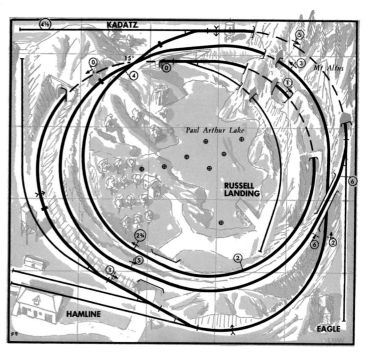

13. Elizabeth & Rahway River Ry. Sharp curves

This type of railroad is easy to put together and lends itself well for window displays, portable table railroads and beginner's projects.

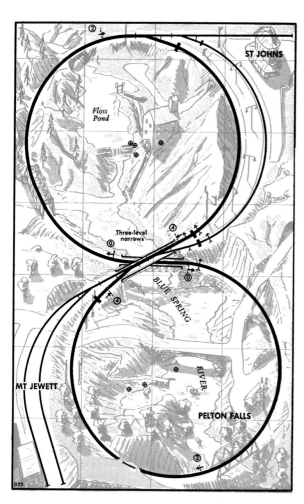

Multiply figured dimen-
sions and elevations by:
½″ for N
¾″ for TT
1″ for HO
1½″ for S
2″ for O
Crossing angle is the
same in all scales.

14. Blue Valley RR. Sharp curves

Figure-eight plans don't look quite as toylike as a simple oval, but either can be vastly improved by good scenery. Here's one of those rarities where one bridge is built above another.

15. Lake District Ry. Adapted from a design by W. R. Budd. Sharp curves

This railroad won a prize in a contest for small railroad plans. We've modified it to use standard sizes of switches. Curves are sharp. The three laps are cleverly arranged to give a long run.

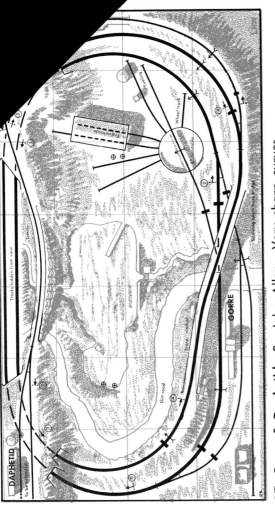

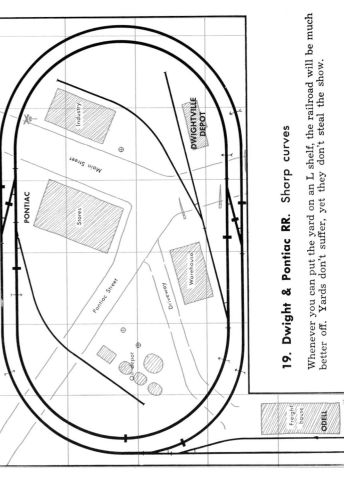

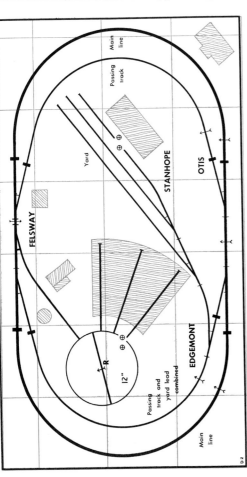

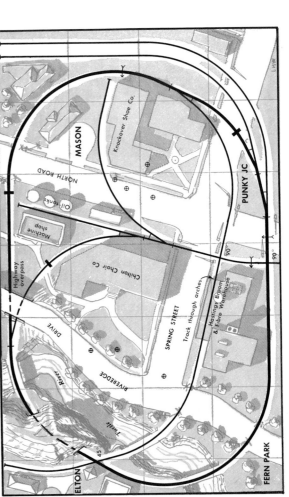

16. Valley Central Lines. Very sharp and sharp curves

This railroad is similar to plan 3, but it isn't as wide. This is accomplished by using very sharp curves, 15" radius, for the inner passing tracks. The remaining curves are the usual 18" radius for this type of plan and turnouts are No. 4.

17. Gorre & Daphetid. By John Allen. Very sharp curves

This name identifies the beginning of what has since become one of the most complicated but finest home model railroads ever built. We've changed the curves to 15" and larger radii; originally they were even sharper. Turnouts are No. 4.

18. Turtle River Industrial District. Sharp curves

Scenery and structures will look good on a plan like this. This type of plan is excellent for the man who wants a good effect without complication.

19. Dwight & Pontiac RR. Sharp curves

Whenever you can put the yard on an L shelf, the railroad will be much better off. Yards don't suffer, yet they don't steal the show.

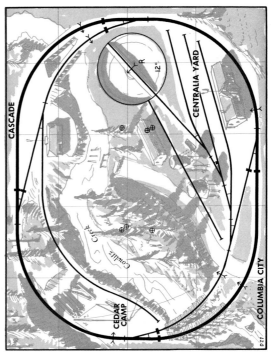

21. Rockport & Oyster Bay RR. Sharp curves

Scenery at the waterfront is the main feature of this otherwise **very** simple railroad plan.

23. Columbia & Cascade RR. Sharp curves

For two-train operation, this is a most compact railroad. The peculiar placement of the passing tracks can be used to save space on other plans.

Multiply figured dimensions and elevations by:
½″ for N
¾″ for TT
1″ for HO
1½″ for S
2″ for O
All plans have No. 4 turnouts.

Ruled lines across plan are:
6″ apart in N
9″ apart in TT
12″ apart in HO
18″ apart in S
24″ apart in O
See page 70 for more data.

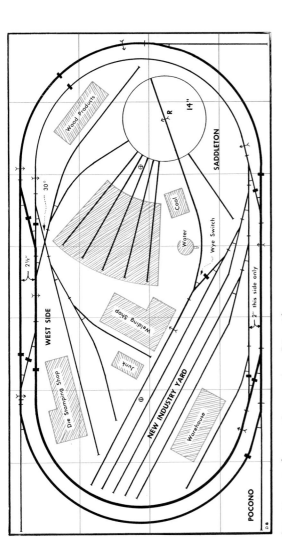

20. New Industry Connecting RR. Sharp curves

Compare this one with plan 18. Here scenery is sacrificed for much more track. There are not many more places to switch, but there is more car and engine capacity at each place. A fine plan for the fellow who builds lots of cars but has only a small space for his railroad.

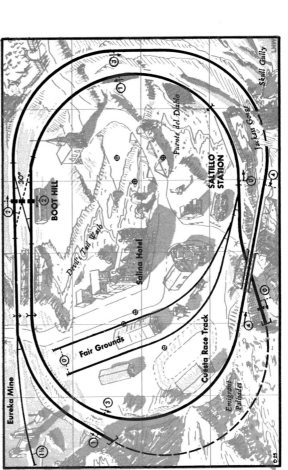

22. Tonopah & Salt Range RR. Sharp curves

Unless there's a mine working somewhere out on the desert, a line like this is likely to fold up anytime. Put trees and grass over the same reddish earth and it will be like an entirely new railroad — might even fool folks at first.

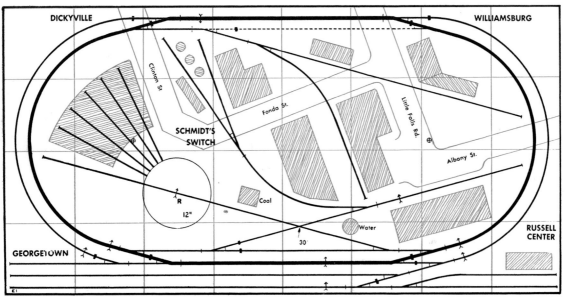

24. Toronto, Hamilton & Detroit RR. Sharp curves

Key labels on map: WOODSTOCK, DUNDAS, LONDON, HAMILTON, INGERSOLL, Albert Canal, BRANTFORD JC, McKenzie Road, DES JARDINS, ST THOMAS, PARIS, 90°, 24" radius, 28½" radius

Multiply figured dimensi
and elevations by:
½" for N
¾" for TT
1" for HO
1½" for S
2" for O
Crossing angle is the sa
all scales.

Ruled lines across plan a
6" apart in N
9" apart in TT
12" apart in HO
18" apart in S
24" apart in O
See page 70 for more da

DICKYVILLE · WILLIAMSBURG · Clinton St. · Fonda St. · Little Falls Rd. · SCHMIDT'S SWITCH · Albany St. · Coal · Water · R 12" · 30' · GEORGETOWN · RUSSELL CENTER

25. Mohawk Southern Ry. Sharp curves

26. Pennsylvania & Potomac RR. By John Armstrong. Sharp curves

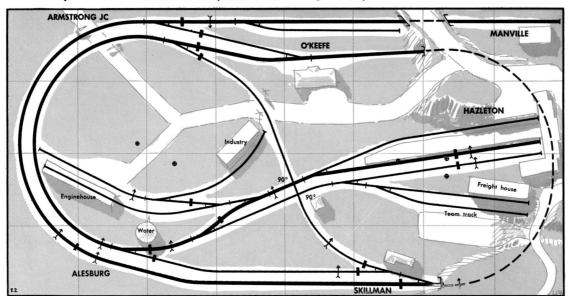

Labels: ARMSTRONG JC, O'KEEFE, MANVILLE, HAZLETON, Industry, Freight house, Enginehouse, 90°, 90°, Team track, Water, ALESBURG, SKILLMAN

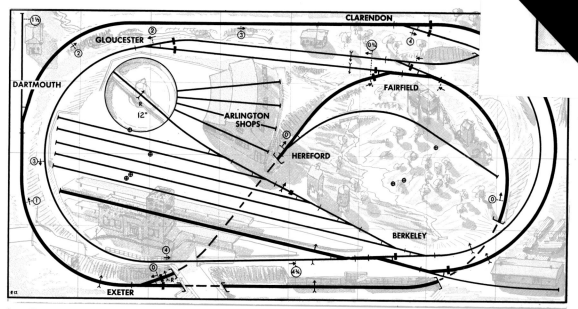

27. Tremont & Cambridge RR. Sharp curves

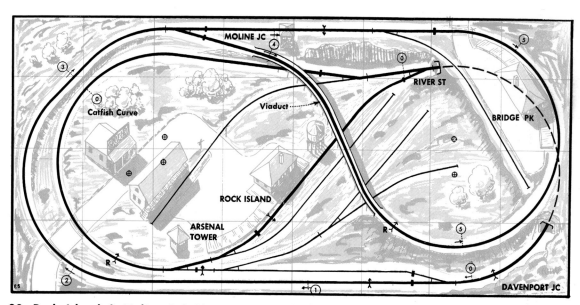

28. Rock Island & Moline Belt Line. By Mark Canum. Sharp curves

29. Nantahala & Smoky Mountain Gorge RR. Sharp curves

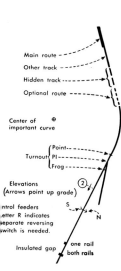

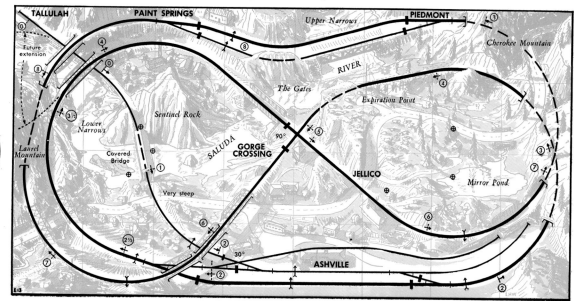

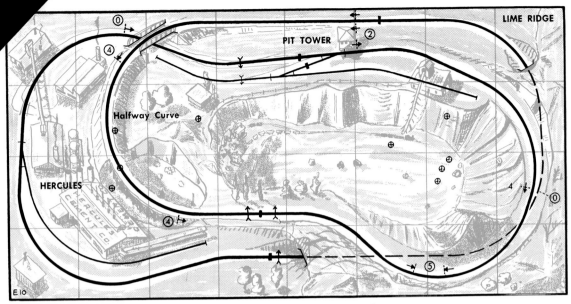

30. Lime Ridge, Hercules & Portland RR. By Bill Wight. Very sharp curves

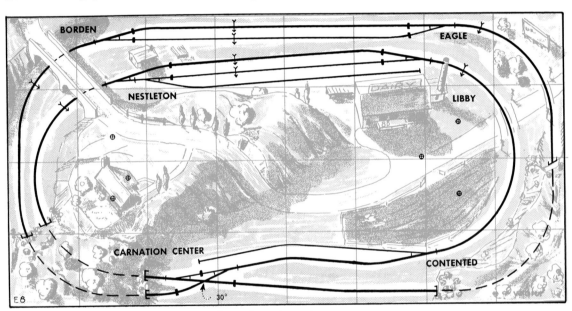

31. Jersey Valley Central RR. By Bill Wight. Very sharp curves

32. Custer & Front Range RR. By Bill Wight. Very sharp curves

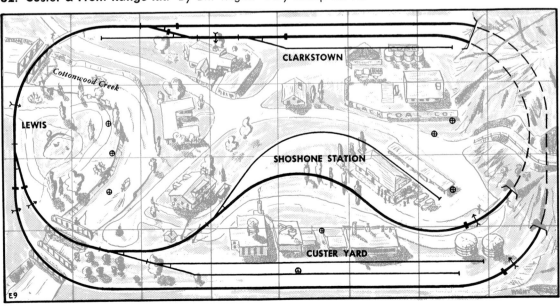

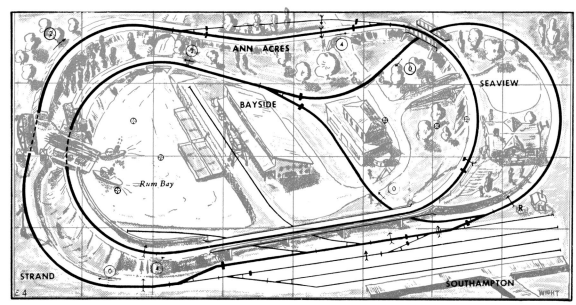

33. Bayside & Southampton Ry. Very sharp curves

Multiply figured dimensions and elevations by:
½″ for N
¾″ for TT
1″ for HO
1½″ for S
2″ for O
Exception:
Elevations in plan 34 are in scale feet for your scale.
Crossing angle is the same in all scales.

Ruled lines across plans are:
6″ apart in N
9″ apart in TT
12″ apart in HO
18″ apart in S
24″ apart in O
Exception:
Plan 34 has double this spacing.
See page 70 for more data.

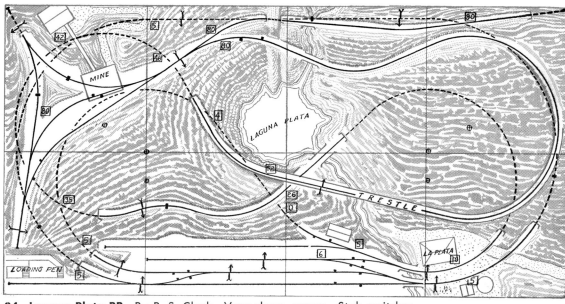

34. Laguna Plata RR. By R. S. Clark. Very sharp curves. Stub switches

35. Denver & South Park RR. By Carroll Weis. Very sharp curves. Stub switches

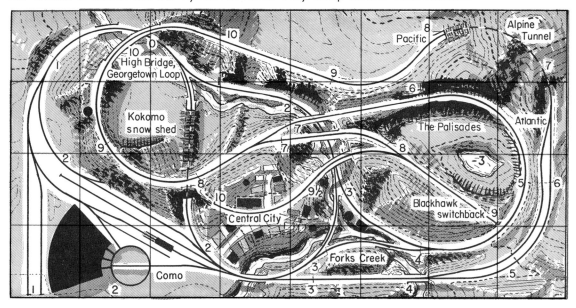

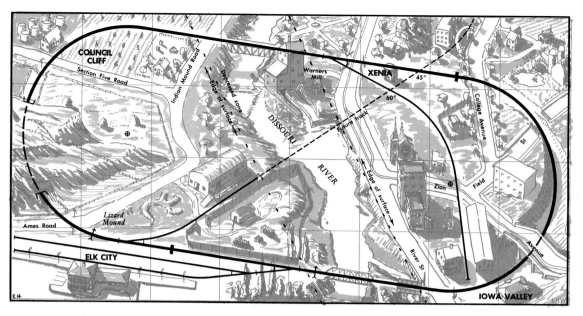

36. Ft. Dodge & Elk City RR. Sharp curves. Easy construction

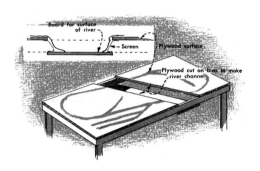

Board for surface of river
Screen
Plywood surface
Plywood cut on bias to make river channel

By cutting a diagonal through the plywood table top and separating the surfaces, a channel is easily made so that some scenic features can be below track level.

Railroads to 6 x 10
Eight plans

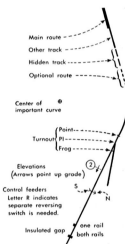

Main route
Other track
Hidden track
Optional route

Center of important curve ⊕

Point
Turnout ⎰ Pl
Frog

Elevations (Arrows point up grade)

Control feeders
Letter R indicates separate reversing switch is needed.

Insulated gap

one rail
both rails

37. Yankee Midland Ry. Very sharp curves

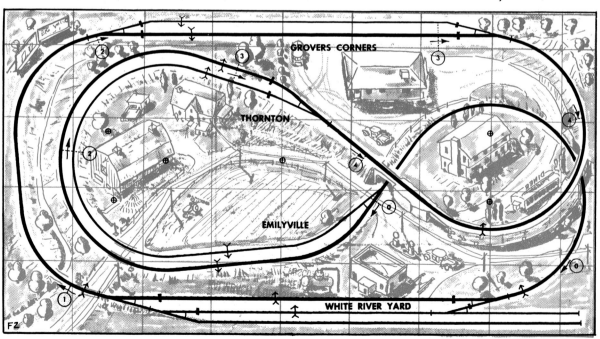

Continued from page 4

get excellent scenic effects on almost any plan, so other factors like the routing of the main line may be more important in choosing a plan even though scenery is your chief interest.

In looking through the plans, you'll find most of them show suggestions for scenery. These ideas are not necessarily wedded to the particular plans on which you find them. You can treat any railroad with many different scenic themes equally well. Decide whether you want desert, mountain, prairie, rural, urban, industrial, timber, mining, waterfront or some other sort of scene without reference to your choice of a track plan. The chances are good that you can carry out your scenic theme on the track arrangement that is most convenient for other reasons.

Are level railroads easier to build than layouts with grades and bridges?

Yes, they're easier to build if you think only of getting track down. It's easy to slap down a sheet of plywood and lay either sectional or built-up track in place. I'd recommend one-level railroads for quick construction.

But you can miss much in the final scenic effect on a one-level railroad. The serious model railroader who wants a fine setting for his trains will be more satisfied if he has the time to

Continued on page 24

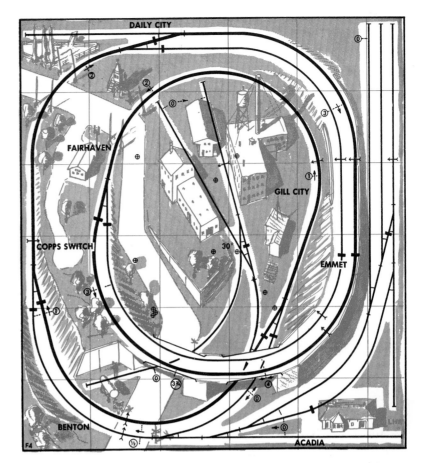

38. Central Missouri RR. Sharp curves

39. Denver & Northwestern RR. Conventional curves

The interesting features of this otherwise rather ordinary plan are the use of a lower (or, if you wish, upper) level for the branch, but with the rest of the railroad on a flat top. Also, the tracks allow for easy expansion of the main lines to the right and the eventual lengthening of yard tracks.

Multiply figured dimensions and elevations by:
- ½″ for N
- ¾″ for TT
- 1″ for HO
- 1½″ for S
- 2″ for O

Crossing angle is the same in all scales.

Ruled lines across plan are:
- 6″ apart in N
- 9″ apart in TT
- 12″ apart in HO
- 18″ apart in S
- 24″ apart in O

See page 70 for more data.

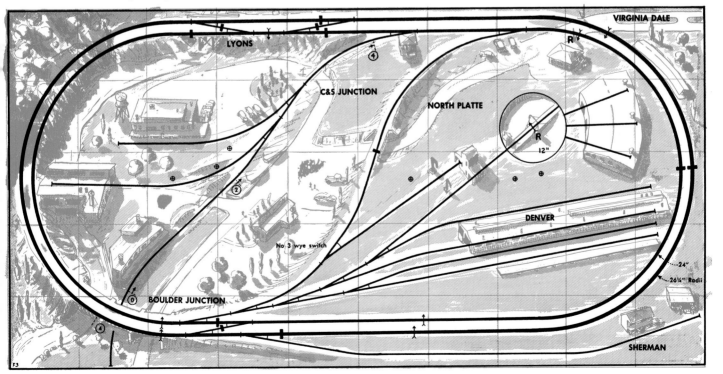

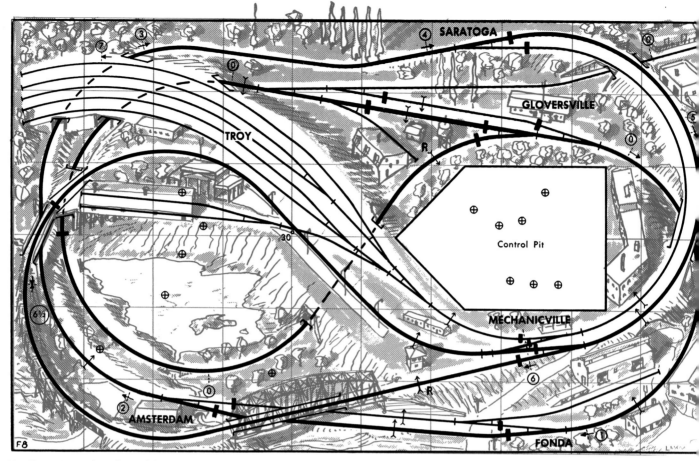

40. Troy & Mohawk Valley Ry. Above. Conventional
curves

Loop-to-loop operation is something like the arrangement of a real railroad, yet it still permits you to run trains for a long time without stopping or backing. A control pit makes this railroad usable where some even smaller plans won't work.

41. Quaker State Eastern RR. Below. Sharp curves

The river divides parallel lines as though they were either competing companies or a new and old route of the same company. It's best to build a river a few inches below track level.

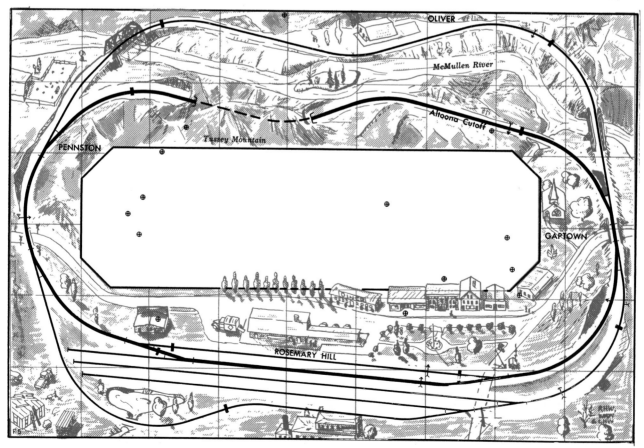

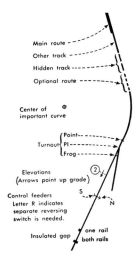

Main route - - - - →
Other track - - - - →
Hidden track - - - - →
Optional route - - - - →

Center of ⊕
important curve

Turnout {
Point - - - - →
PI - - - - →
Frog - - - - →
}

Elevations
(Arrows point up grade)

Control feeders
Letter R indicates
separate reversing
switch is needed.

Insulated gap { one rail both rails }

Multiply figured dimensions and elevations by:
½″ for N
¾″ for TT
1″ for HO
1½″ for S
2″ for O
Crossing angle is the same in all scales.

Ruled lines across plan are:
6″ apart in N
9″ apart in TT
12″ apart in HO
18″ apart in S
24″ apart in O
See page 70 for more data.

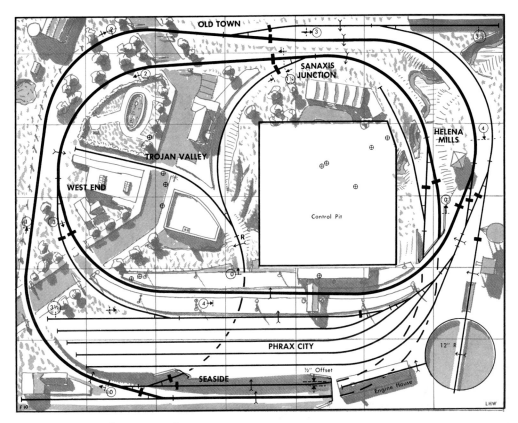

42. Sanaxis & Phrax RR. Sharp curves

The offset in track alignment, lower right, saves space. It allows the straight tracks to be closer together than could be permitted around sharp curves.

43. Deadwood, Big Horn & Pacific RR. Sharp curves

Here's another one of those fascinating railroads that winds its way up a mountainside. Compare it with plans 34, 44, 63, 75, 78, 86, 95, and 96.

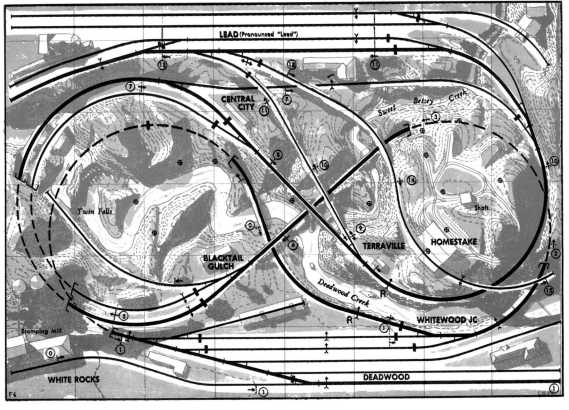

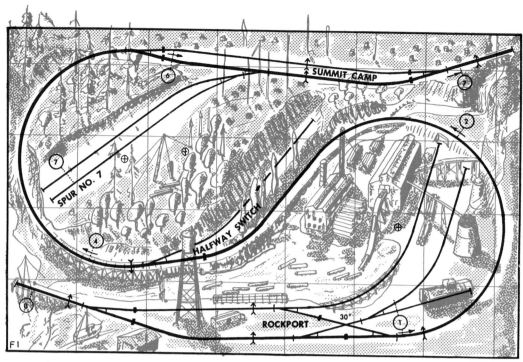

Railroads up to 9 x 12

Fourteen plans

44. Rockport & South Fork Lumber Co. Sharp curves

I've been to several real places called Rockport and I think every one of them was a most interesting small seaport. Here a lumber mill ships its wares while a simple railroad brings timber down from the camp. Downhill trains go into a single-ended siding to let uphill trains go by.

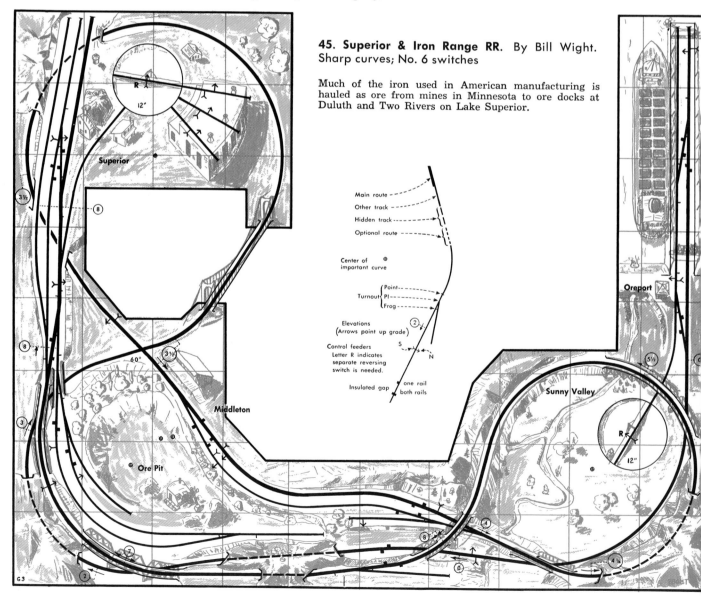

45. Superior & Iron Range RR. By Bill Wight. Sharp curves; No. 6 switches

Much of the iron used in American manufacturing is hauled as ore from mines in Minnesota to ore docks at Duluth and Two Rivers on Lake Superior.

Main route ----
Other track ----
Hidden track ----
Optional route ----

Center of ⊕
important curve

Turnout { Point----
{ Pl----
{ Frog----

Elevations
(Arrows point up grade)

Control feeders
Letter R indicates
separate reversing
switch is needed.

Insulated gap { one rail
{ both rails

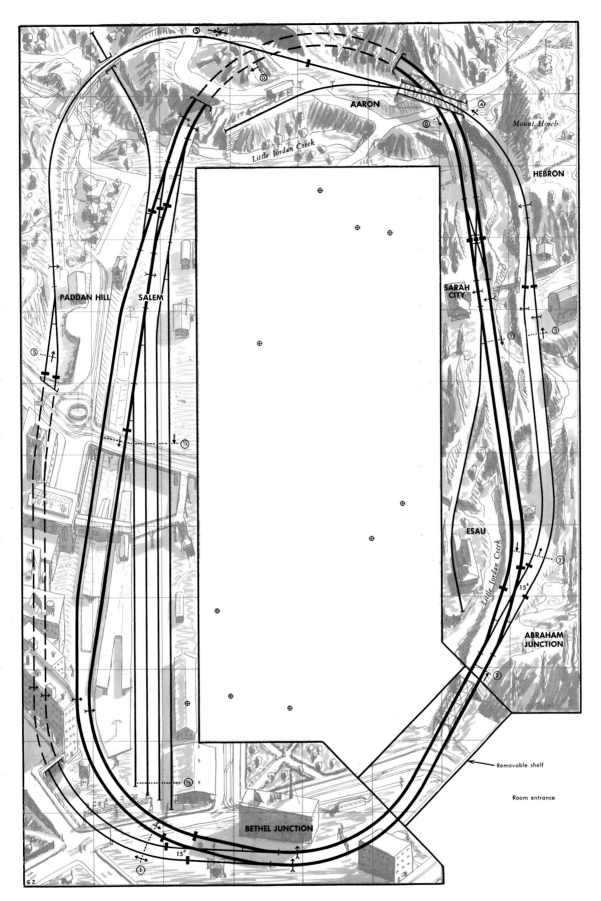

Little Jordan Creek

AARON

Mount Horeb

HEBRON

PADDAN HILL   SALEM

SARAH CITY

ESAU

Little Jordan Creek

ABRAHAM JUNCTION

15°

Removable shelf

Room entrance

BETHEL JUNCTION

15°

46. Jordan Valley RR. Conventional curves

Here again a river helps to separate parallel tracks. On the left side the second line is hidden behind buildings.

Multiply figured dimensions and elevations by:

½″ for N
¾″ for TT
1″ for HO
1½″ for S
2″ for O

Crossing angle is the same in all scales.

Ruled lines across plan are:

6″ apart in N
9″ apart in TT
12″ apart in HO
18″ apart in S
24″ apart in O

See page 70 for more data.

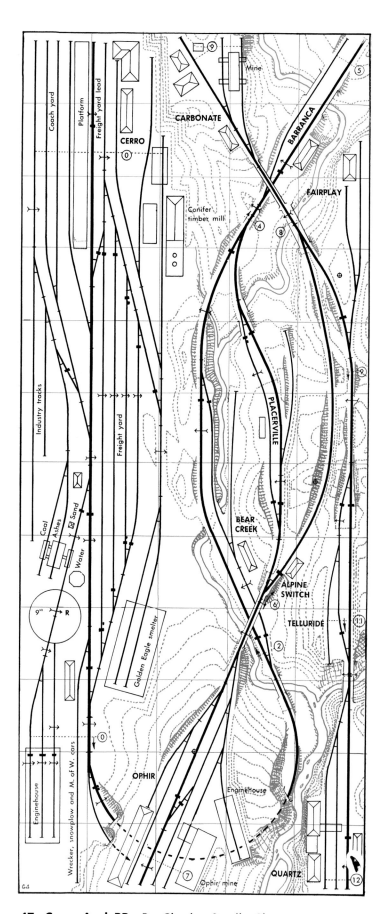

47. Cerro Azul RR. By Charles Small. Sharp curves

This is one of my favorites of the switchback type of plan. Charles Small shows his knowledge of mining railroads and the influence of his experiences in South America in this plan, but it might be just as much at home in a Colorado or Idaho setting.

Continued from page 19

build a grid-type table with track at various levels. Books like *Practical Guide to Model Railroading* and *Scenery for Model Railroads* show how this is done; it's easier than you think once you actually start work.

Railroads that can be built on one level: 3, 4, 10, 11, 12, 13, 16, 18, 19, 20, 21, 23, 25, 26, 31, 32, 36, 41, 55, 56, 68, 71, 72, 76 (first stage only), 81, 83, 87, 89. Also, except for the branch line: 5, 39, 49, 69, and 91.

Will the curves handle all sizes of locomotives?

The curves for each plan are marked very sharp, sharp, conventional, or broad. Sharp curves are those commonly used with No. 4 track switches. Conventional curves are one third larger in radius and are usually used with No. 6 turnouts. Broad curves are at least a quarter larger, nearly double the radius of sharp curves.

You can run any kind of equipment on broad curves. Conventional curves will handle all but the largest locomotives. Passenger cars can be operated around conventional curves, but only shortened passenger cars will look right. Sharp curves will handle medium-sized locomotives and some large ones. Passenger cars don't look good on sharp curves. Very sharp curves are used on industrial lines, trolley layouts, and for tricky model railroads such as those built under a coffee-table glass. They usually require homemade or specially made switches. A very thorough discussion of curves can be found in the book *Practical Guide to Model Railroading*; this book also lists the radii that many commercially made locomotives can negotiate.

Aren't your turntables too small?

Could be. We have tried not to use big turntables on railroads where small locomotives are at home. But many model railroaders like big locos regardless. In most plans you can substitute almost any size of turntable for the one we show.

Are some plans better for my scale than others?

Whether in O, S, HO, TT, or N, the operation of any of these plans is the same. However, there is a difference because of the space you need to stand in, and the reach of your arm. In plan 93, there's a space next to the roundhouse where a fellow can stand to operate the main terminal and the

Continued on page 36

Ruled lines across plan are:
  6" apart in N
  9" apart in TT
  12" apart in HO
  18" apart in S
  24" apart in O
See page 70 for more data.

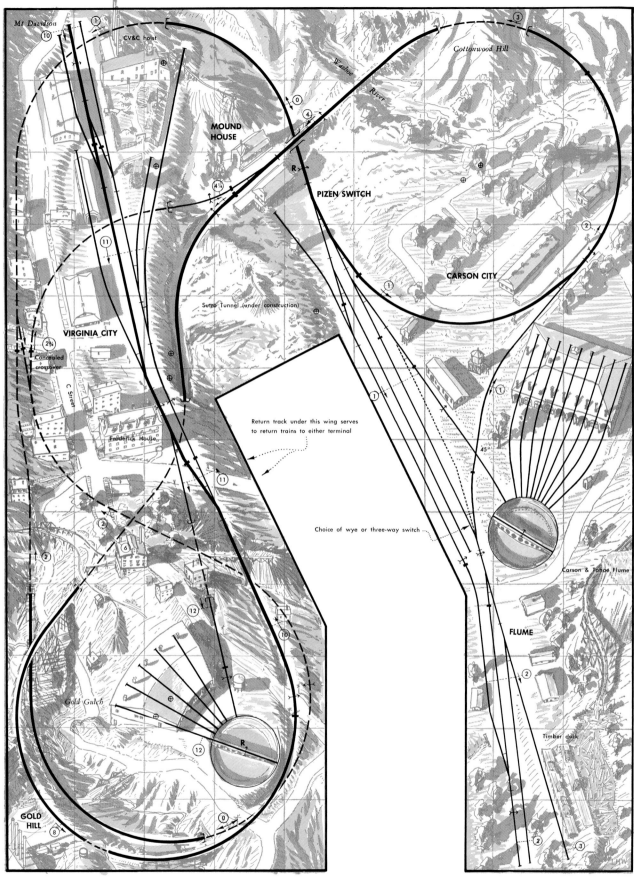

48. Virginia & Truckee RR. Conventional curves

Much of the now abandoned and once fabulous V&T is recaptured here. The track arrangement could also fit well with other railroad themes. The conventional radius curves and No. 6 switches will take any locomotive. Some model railroaders will want to add a few more tracks in the two yards.

Multiply figured dimensions
and elevations by:
½″ for N
¾″ for TT
1″ for HO
1½″ for S
2″ for O
Crossing angle is the same in
all scales.

49. Fairhaven & Ideal River RR.
By Billi Bowen. Conventional curves. Custom switches

Ideal Models built this layout to display the structures they sell. It has since been dismantled, but was on display for several years. Notice how circular curves are connected, not by straight track, but by easy curves laid by eye. You can do this to improve almost any plan for scenic purposes.

Dummy track or future extension

13" R

G6

Multiply figured dimensions and elevations by:

½" for N
¾" for TT
1" for HO
1½" for S
2" for O

Ruled lines across plan are:

6" apart in N
9" apart in TT
12" apart in HO
18" apart in S
24" apart in O
See page 70 for more data.

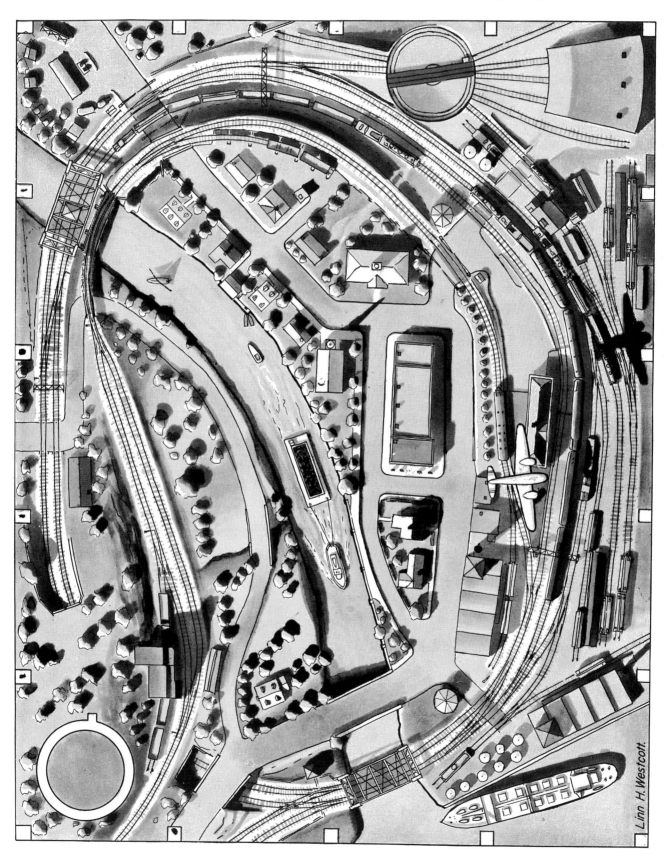

Linn H. Westcott.

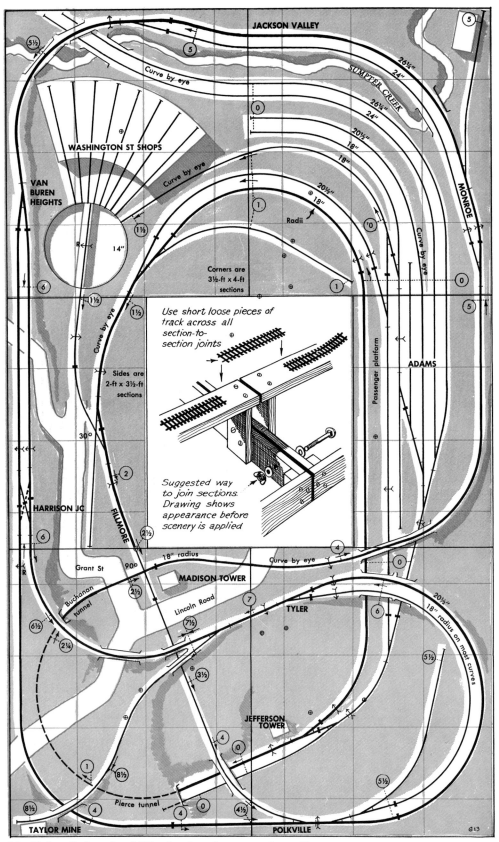

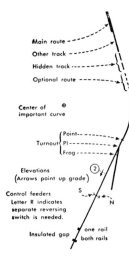

Main route - - - - -
Other track - - - - -
Hidden track - - - - -
Optional route - - - - -

Center of ⊕
important curve

Turnout { Point - - - -
Pl - - - -
Frog - - - -

Elevations
(Arrows point up grade)

Control feeders
Letter R indicates
separate reversing
switch is needed.

Insulated gap / one rail
both rails

Multiply figured dimen-
sions and elevations by:
½″ for N
¾″ for TT
1″ for HO
1½″ for S
2″ for O
Crossing angle is the
same in all scales.

Ruled lines across plan are:
6″ apart in N
9″ apart in TT
12″ apart in HO
18″ apart in S
24″ apart in O
See page 70 for more data.

50. Union & Overland RR. Sectional construction. Sharp curves

I once built a railroad in six pieces that bolted together to make a
10 x 12-foot layout. The plan of this was published and it became
one of the top railroads in popularity. Along the same line of reason-
ing, I worked out this railroad with the idea of getting just as much
operation into a smaller space. I have tried to include an adequate
yard, scenic areas, interesting junctions, a crossing, and places to
build factories on spurs. As on the original sectional plan, you can
add more sections to fill a large space. See plan 61 for one possibility.

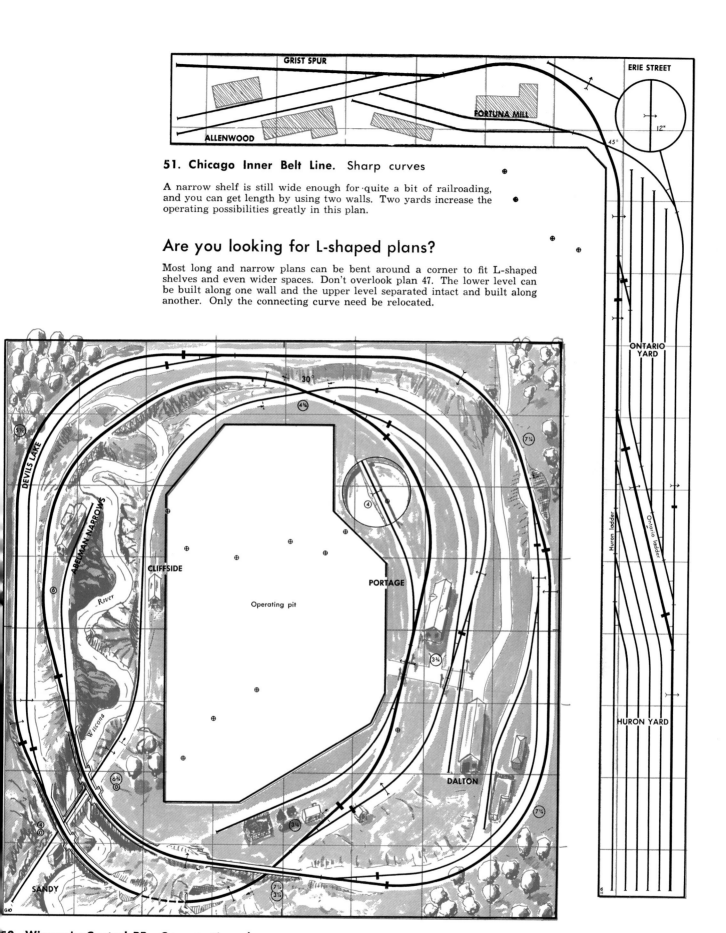

51. Chicago Inner Belt Line. Sharp curves

A narrow shelf is still wide enough for quite a bit of railroading, and you can get length by using two walls. Two yards increase the operating possibilities greatly in this plan.

Are you looking for L-shaped plans?

Most long and narrow plans can be bent around a corner to fit L-shaped shelves and even wider spaces. Don't overlook plan 47. The lower level can be built along one wall and the upper level separated intact and built along another. Only the connecting curve need be relocated.

52. Wisconsin Central RR. Conventional curves

In a square room, the arrangement of track is hampered by lack of distance between the corner curves. This plan makes the best of it with a two-lap oval and a branch line.

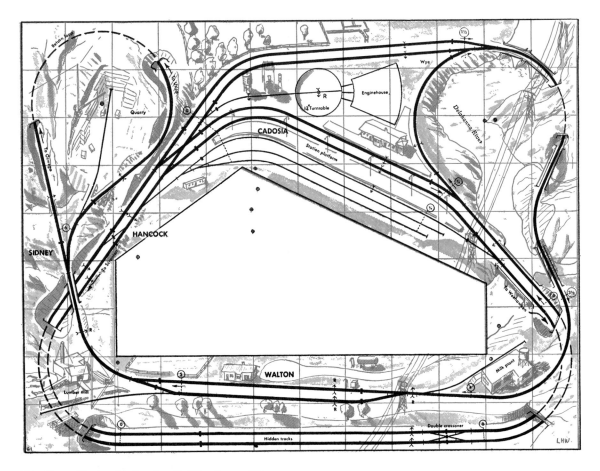

53. New York, Ontario & Western RR.
Sharp curves

The double-track oval serves as a mileage maker. Most of the operating interest will be in the yard and on the branch line.

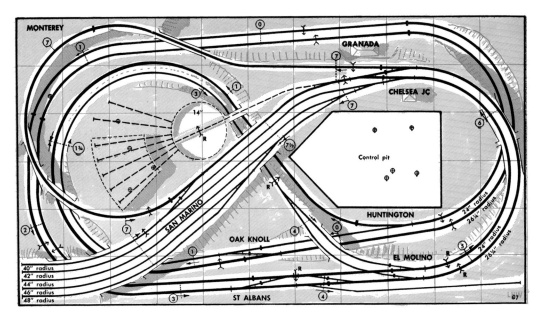

54. San Marino & Echo Mountain Ry. Conventional curves

This is about the average of the sizes of model railroad actually built. Here a plan often used on a 4 x 8 table is expanded to take a little more space.

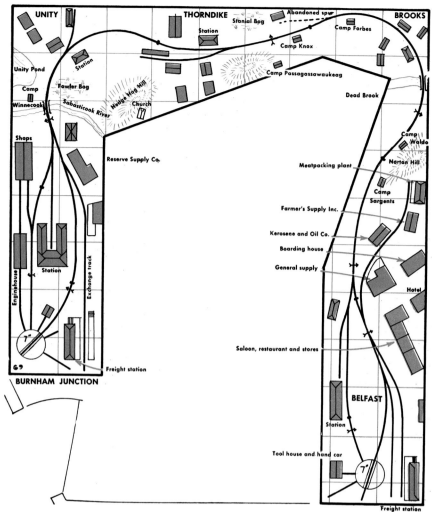

55. Belfast & Moosehead Lake RR. By J. D. Latham Jr.
Sharp curves and stub switches

This and plan 53 are based upon real railroads in
the East. The B&ML is a line from a seaport to
the main line of the Maine Central.

Main route - - - -
Other track - - - - -
Hidden track - - - - →
Optional route - - - - -

Center of ⊕
important curve

Turnout
Pt
Point - - - - -
Pl - - - - -
Frog - - - - -

Elevations
(Arrows point up grade)
②
S
N

Control feeders
Letter R indicates
separate reversing
switch is needed.

Insulated gap
one rail
both rails

Multiply figured dimen-
sions and elevations by:
½″ for N
¾″ for TT
1″ for HO
1½″ for S
2″ for O
Crossing angle is the
same in all scales.

Ruled lines across plan are:
6″ apart in N
9″ apart in TT
12″ apart in HO
18″ apart in S
24″ apart in O
See page 70 for more data.

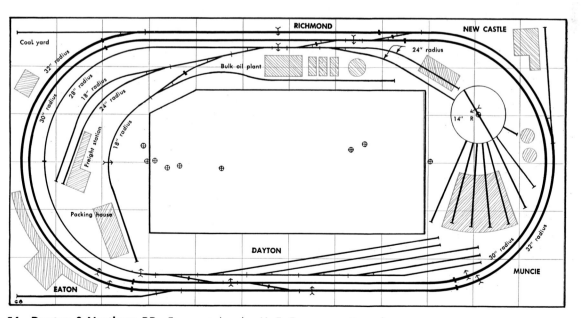

56. Dayton & Northern RR. From a plan by H. F. Freeman. Broad curves

Here's a small railroad suited to the man who
wants to test the largest locomotives and have a
little operating fun as well.

Railroads for 12 x 16 spaces

(Except plan 60 which is
4½ x 11.)

57. Baltimore & Hudson RR. Conventional curves

58. Grand River Western RR. (Opposite page.) Conventional curves

When the feature "Layout of the Month" was first running in Model Railroader, one plan showed a way to add return loops and a better yard to a double-track oval. This plan became the most popular of all model track plans. Here it is revised to take a little less space, above, or a little more space, below. Notice that the main line is not level. This makes the loop grades much easier. The lower plan was developed from the upper by the scissors method explained on page 40. Notes in color show the changes that were made. This same idea is an easy way to enlarge any other plan you might like.

Note. Entire outer oval is wired as a return track. This makes operation easy over crossovers as well as in loop-to-loop arrangement.

EASTON — RIVER JC — YORK JC — HUDSON JC — YORK — BALTIMORE — LANCASTER CROSSING — M&P JC — BERGEN — VALLEY FORGE — MORNINGSIDE DEPTHS — OWSON JC

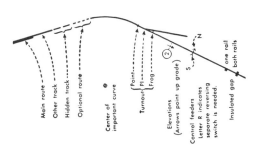

Main route
Other track
Hidden track
Optional route
Center of important curve
Turnout { Point / Pl / Frog }
Elevations (Arrows point up grade)
Control feeders Letter R indicates separate reversing switch is needed.
Insulated gap { one rail / both rails }

Multiply figured dimensions
and elevations by:
½" for N
¾" for TT
1" for HO
1½" for S
2" for O
Crossing angle is the same in
all scales.

Ruled lines across plan are:
6" apart in N
9" apart in TT
12" apart in HO
18" apart in S
24" apart in O
See page 70 for more data.

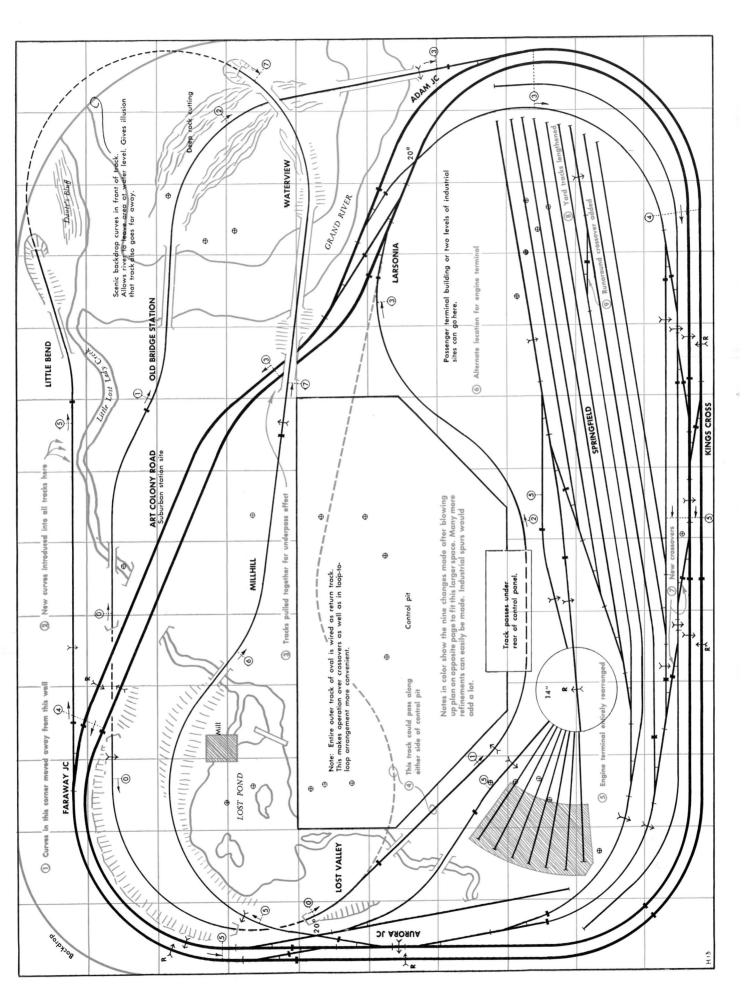

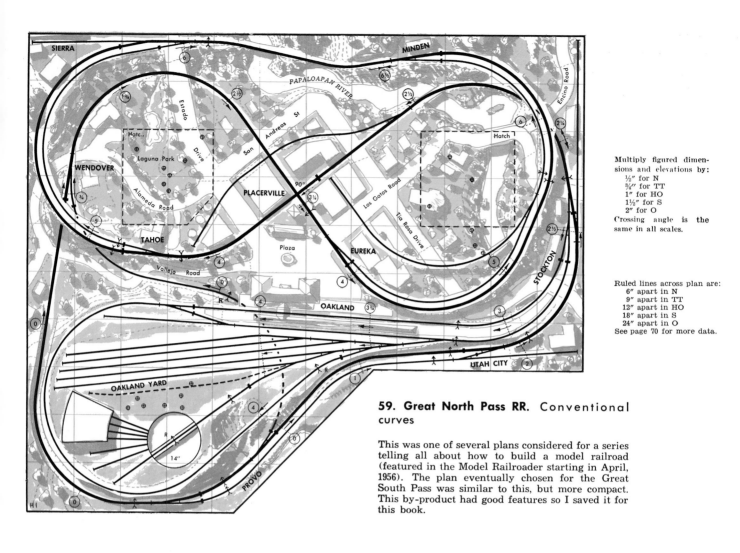

Multiply figured dimensions and elevations by:
½″ for N
¾″ for TT
1″ for HO
1½″ for S
2″ for O
Crossing angle is the same in all scales.

Ruled lines across plan are:
6″ apart in N
9″ apart in TT
12″ apart in HO
18″ apart in S
24″ apart in O
See page 70 for more data.

59. Great North Pass RR. Conventional curves

This was one of several plans considered for a series telling all about how to build a model railroad (featured in the Model Railroader starting in April, 1956). The plan eventually chosen for the Great South Pass was similar to this, but more compact. This by-product had good features so I saved it for this book.

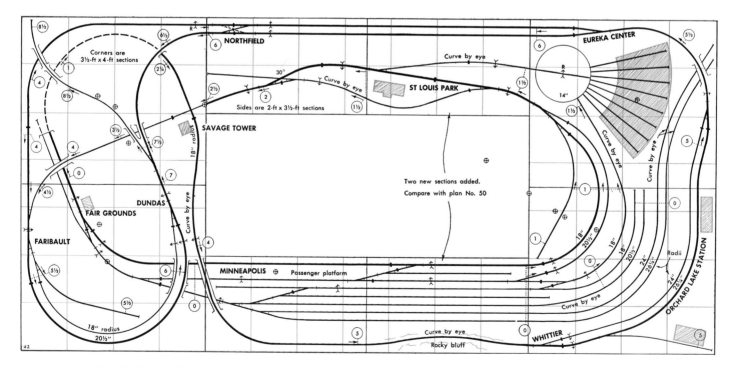

61. Dan Patch Lines. Sharp Curves

More yard capacity is provided in this plan than in the original from which it grew, plan 50. One advantage of building a railroad in sections is that you can build on the workbench where tools are handy. You can make alterations the same way even after the entire railroad is completed.

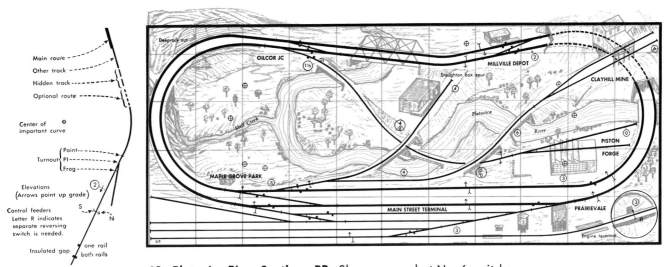

Main route ---→
Other track ----→
Hidden track -----→
Optional route -----→

Center of   ⊕
important curve

Turnout {
  Point----→
  Pl ----→
  Frog ----→
}

Elevations   ②
(Arrows point up grade)

Control feeders
Letter R indicates
separate reversing
switch is needed.

Insulated gap {
  one rail
  both rails
}

60. Platonica River Southern RR. Sharp curves but No. 6 switches

The ordinary effect of a simple oval is broken by putting the spurs at different elevations.

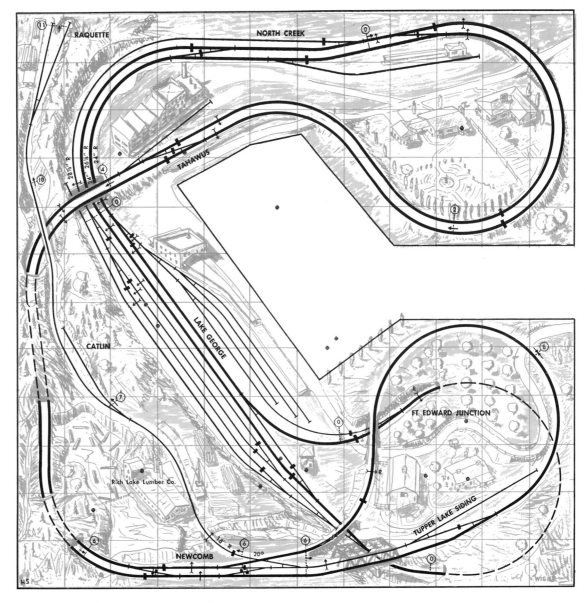

62. Adirondack RR. Conventional curves

Another popular plan from years ago. In one version it was called the "New York, New Haven & Hollywood." Besides offering a good main line, the branch increases the operating interest.

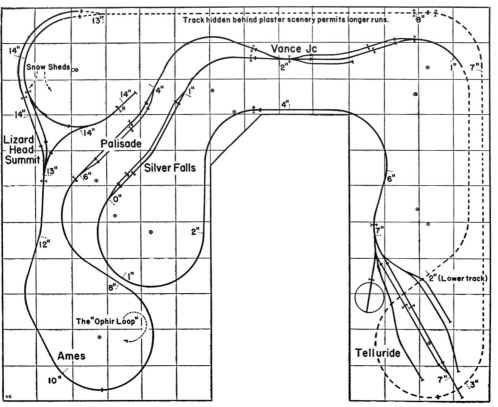

13"
14"
Snow Sheds
14"
Lizard Head Summit
Palisade
14"
4"
1"
R
14"
13"
6"
Silver Falls
0"
2"
12"
1"
8"
The "Ophir Loop"
Ames
10"

Track hidden behind plaster scenery permits longer runs.
Vance Jc
2"
4"
8"
7"
1"
6"
7"
2" (Lower track)
Telluride
7"
3"

H6

63. Rio Grande Southern Ry. Sharp curves. Stub switches

Probably more beautiful photos of a railroad scene have been taken near the Ophir Loop on the Rio Grande Southern than anywhere else in America. Now the real railroad is gone, but you can rebuild it in model form. This plan uses stub switches but No. 4 switches will fit with little or no change of track alignment. The left side of this railroad could be fitted into many other shapes of rooms by completely revising the right side.

Multiply figured dimensions and elevations by:
½" for N
¾" for TT
1" for HO
1½" for S
2" for O

Continued from page 24

engine terminal. This railroad was originally built in O gauge. If built in HO, the cockpit would be so small you couldn't stand in it. You need at least an 18"-square hole to stand in, and that's not big enough for a control panel too. The answer here, if you're working in a smaller scale, is to adjust things so you can build a larger control pit. You might have to move the roundhouse somewhere else or even omit it.

Most plans were designed with HO convenience in mind, so the S gauger and O gauger will have to look out for another hazard, that of having to reach too far from the edge of the table to get at some important place. Four feet is about as far as you can reach, and that's the limit. Look for a place to build another hatch for easier access or else move tracks around to make room for a hatch.

How do I choose a plan for an irregularly shaped space?

There are two good ways. The easiest way is to choose a plan that will fit into part of your space and then expand portions of the railroad into the extra areas. You do this by swinging one or several tracks sideways into the widened space, by moving a yard to an outside location (very likely an improvement), by swinging a track into an L or T so far that it makes a horseshoe or hairpin curve, by adding a branch line with many scenic industries, villages or resorts

Ruled lines across plan are:
6" apart in N
9" apart in TT
12" apart in HO
18" apart in S
24" apart in O
See page 70 for more data.

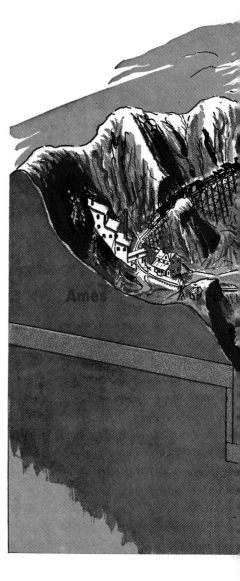

Ames

along the new space, and so on. I'll give you more help on relocating track later.

The other way is to take a plan of about the proper area and bend it, stretch it, squeeze it or pinch it narrow at the middle. This takes more revising, but the method I'm going to describe of cutting a tracing of the plan into four corners and then relocating them is good for this.

More pointers about choosing your track plan

The most important thing to consider in making your choice is the arrangement of the main line. Is it long enough? Does it make an interesting journey for the trains?

Even though a particular plan doesn't have what you want in yards, scenery, spurs or other details, if the main line is right you've probably found the best layout for your needs.

Scenery can always be changed. In fact, you can treat almost any plan in a thousand different ways when it comes to adding scenery.

Spurs can also be changed. You can add more, take some away, run others in different directions. Lots of fellows don't build spurs until later on anyway, and that's an idea that has some merit.

Passing sidings can also be moved. Likewise, you can change double track to single track or vice versa.

Yards aren't quite as flexible, but in almost any plan there are at least two places where yards could be located, so even here you have a choice. Look at yards on other plans; often you can make a substitution more to your liking.

We've tried to keep the yards in the plans to about the right sizes for the main lines they serve. However, most fellows eventually acquire more cars than they can use. If you're one of them, you'll either have to add more yard tracks somewhere, or else build a wall display case for extra equipment so the layout doesn't get yard-heavy.

Many plans that have been published have wasted trackage that is added for effect without consideration of how trains will operate. One test of a good operating plan is that a train should go over practically all mainline track before repeating any of it. Alternate routes and cutoffs which connect into the main at two places usually are of little use and merely clutter up space. There sometimes are good reasons for having these cutoffs, but I'm criticizing plans that have a jumble of trackage that connects into itself here and there without ever really getting anywhere.

Branch lines are another thing. A branch line adds a lot of operating interest. Usually it works out best if it ties into the main line at only one place, at a point fairly well away from the main terminal. This makes for longer running.

Check your aisles and operating spaces.

Many plans require some space outside the main tables for standing room.

Continued on page 68

Multiply figured dimensions and elevations by:
½″ for N
¾″ for TT
1″ for HO
1½″ for S
2″ for O
Crossing angle is the same in all scales.

Continued from page 9

our location a bad choice, you can usually change the location of a yard to many other arrangements without changing much of the main line. The safest way to do this is to keep a yard attached to the main track at the same place, but swing it in another direction or build it on the other side of the main line.

To entirely relocate a yard, trace the plan without its yard. Then it will be easier to visualize all the new places where a yard can be built.

When you attach the yard to the main line at a new place, take a look at the return loops. In most plans the loops were located so you could get a maximum run before returning to the yard. To retain this feature, you'll have to move the place where the loops connect to the main line as well as the yard connecting point. We mentioned this long-run feature on page 3.

Factory spurs and other one-ended side tracks can be connected almost anywhere on any plan, so feel free to move them around, add more, take some away, etc. Keep in mind the limitation of cutting a No. 6 switch into a curve, as will be mentioned later.

Curves near the corners of the space and near other tracks are easily moved as long as you can still keep

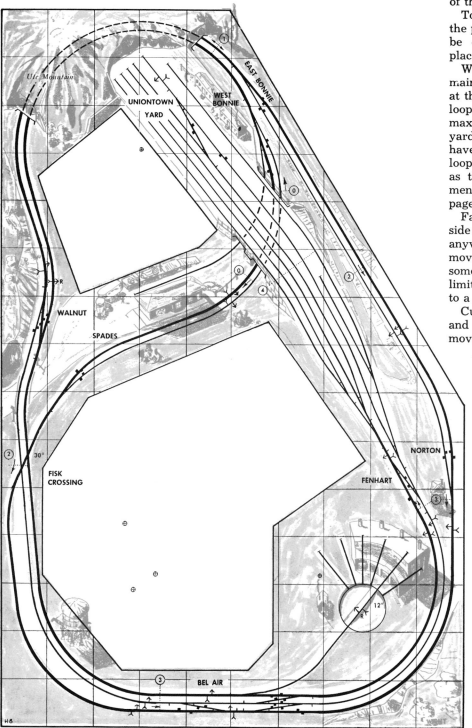

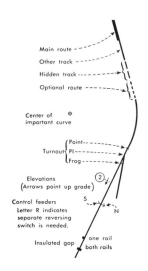

Main route
Other track
Hidden track
Optional route

Center of important curve

Turnout { Point
PI
Frog }

Elevations (Arrows point up grade)

Control feeders
Letter R indicates separate reversing switch is needed.

Insulated gap
one rail
both rails

Ruled lines across plan are:
6″ apart in N
9″ apart in TT
12″ apart in HO
18″ apart in S
24″ apart in O
See page 70 for more data.

64. Uniontown Southern RR. By Bill Wight. Broad curves

For two-train operation, this railroad has a serious flaw that can easily be corrected. As it stands, it's impossible to run two trains continuously in opposite directions as there is only one siding where they can pass (at Norton-East Bonnie). Any attempt to pass on the left half of the railroad is bound to send at least one train into the terminal. To correct this, a right-hand crossover is needed between tracks two and three (counting inward), just to the left of the other crossovers at Bel Air. Track three between this point and Walnut then becomes a second passing siding.

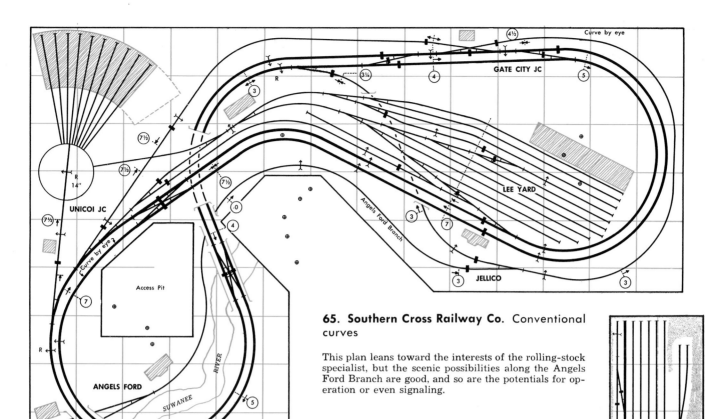

65. Southern Cross Railway Co. Conventional curves

This plan leans toward the interests of the rolling-stock specialist, but the scenic possibilities along the Angels Ford Branch are good, and so are the potentials for operation or even signaling.

66. Eureka, Shasta & Great Eastern Ry. By Bill Wight. Broad curves

Here's a lot of space for scenery; you could follow many different themes equally well. Rivers and bridges wouldn't necessarily have to follow these particular routes.

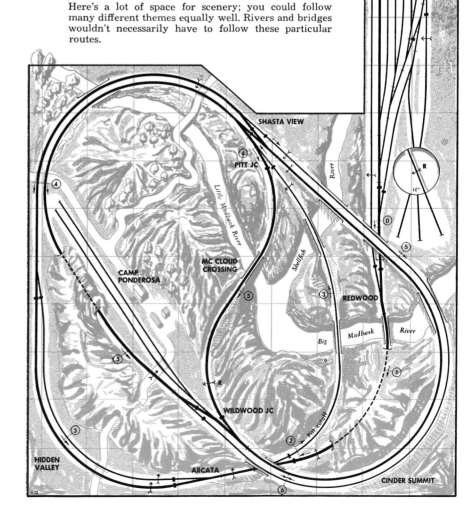

the tracks from getting too close to each other or to the table edge.

A packet of tracing paper and a pencil can be used to combine parts of different plans quickly and safely. There's a track-planning template in the back of the book *Practical Guide to Model Railroading.* It can be a big help in replanning part or all of a plan. Another way is to trace parts of one plan in this book and then fit them to parts of another plan that uses the same radii and scale of drawing.

How can I build a plan that's just a little too large for my space?

Can you build a drop leaf or removable section so that part of your railroad will be out of the way when not in use? If this won't work, you'll have to build the plan smaller. Sometimes you can move the corner curves inward and make new connecting tracks. This won't work on most plans for small spaces because we've already made the plans about as small as possible.

Changing to curves of a shorter radius saves a little space, but not as much as is often needed. If the plan has No. 6 switches, changing to No. 4 switches will save considerable space wherever switches are grouped. Building special switches with a curve all the way through them also saves space. Atlas Snap-Track switches

Continued on next page

Continued from page 39

have a curve of this sort. You can use them in place of standard switch designs, but they won't help much unless you also lop off the extra 1½" of straight track ahead of the points on these switches.

Building part of one switch overlapped into the space of the next is another way to save space. Slip switches and three-way switches are common forms of overlapped switches, but you can make many other unusual switches to save space.

Leaving out part of a plan also helps. Or you can change from double track to single track, omit an entire lap of the main line, leave out the roundhouse, etc.

How can I make the best use of extra space around the plan?

If your railroad space is bigger than the plan calls for, you're well off because almost any plan can be improved by a little expansion. Sometimes just leaving more space around the outer tracks is the best thing you can do. Tilting a plan diagonally in a space creates triangular corners for scenery and may improve an otherwise stiff-looking oval.

A very good way to expand a plan into a larger space is to make a tracing of the original plan, then cut through it each way. Paste the four corners you made into the corners of an outline drawing of your new larger space. Make new connections between the corners and your new expanded plan is done. Compare plan 57 with plan 58 for this is just what I did here.

If the plan you like has sharp curves and No. 4 switches, consider changing to conventional curves and No. 6 switches. This will take up a foot or so of your extra length and improve operation as well.

If your mainline has only two passing sidings, see if you can work in three by moving them around a little. Three is much better for two-train operation.

More yard trackage is always welcome. You can lengthen all yard tracks. If you need still more yardage, you can add more switches to the ladder or build another ladder on the other side of the main line. If you lengthen yard tracks, you may want to lengthen sidings as well as they must hold the same trains.

With quite a bit of extra space, you can consider adding a trolley line, a branch line, or perhaps an extra lap of main line for longer running.

One more way to enlarge a plan is to spread the whole railroad proportionately. Consider the squares as larger than originally intended. For

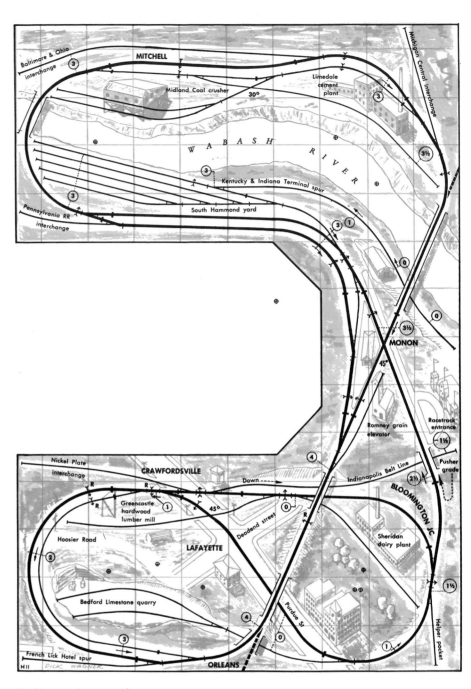

67. Monon Route. Sharp curves

If you're familiar with the real Monon, you'll have fun with this plan. Otherwise you might want to use the track arrangement for some other theme. Some might want to use the Wabash River space to enlarge the yard.

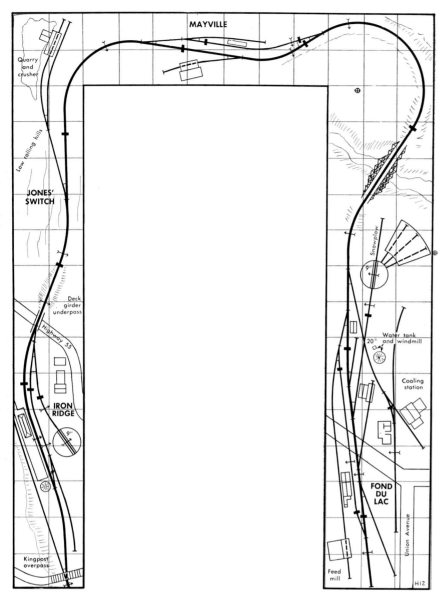

68. Iron Ridge & Mayville. By Paul Larson. Conventional curves

Here's a honey of a point-to-point railroad for the fellow who wants to have the utmost in a realistic effect. The theme is a Milwaukee Road branch line.

instance, in HO the squares might represent 15″ instead of 12″. This would make a railroad with curves of 25 per cent greater radii; the overall size of the plan would also be 25 per cent greater. Use the same size of track switch and figure switch locations by the P.I.F. method on page 7. Double track and yard tracks should not be spread when you use this method. Keep the original center-to-center distances.

Can I change a plan with a single-track main line to double track?

This is fairly easy, but if your space is small you may need a few inches more in length and width than the original plan. Use the same curve centers and add a second track on the outside of the original mainline curves. If this pushes into the territory of another track, you'll have to move the next track out of the way.

This method will change the direction of straight trackage in reverse curves, which does no harm.

Compare plans 84 and 85. These are single-track and double-track versions of the same theme.

Can I substitute No. 8 switches for the No. 6 size shown in many plans?

Usually there isn't enough room for a substitution except in the biggest rooms. No. 8 switches take half again as much length as No. 6, and while they look nice they are not needed even for operating at speed.

Can I add switches where the plans don't show them?

You can almost always cut a switch into an already existing straight track, but cutting a switch into a curve calls for a little caution. A regular No. 4 switch corresponds roughly to a radius a little larger than the curves it is usually used with (about 22″ radius in HO for example). A No. 6 is a lot broader, however (about 48″ radius in HO). So, particularly with a No. 6 switch, it's difficult and often impossible to cut a switch into an existing curve without introducing kinks that are just asking for car derailments. If you cannot relocate track centers to provide for a regular switch, build a custom switch with a curve through the frog.

Multiply figured dimensions and elevations by:
½″ for N
¾″ for TT
1″ for HO
1½″ for S
2″ for O
Crossing angle is the same in all scales.

Ruled lines across plan are:
6″ apart in N
9″ apart in TT
12″ apart in HO
18″ apart in S
24″ apart in O
See page 70 for more data.

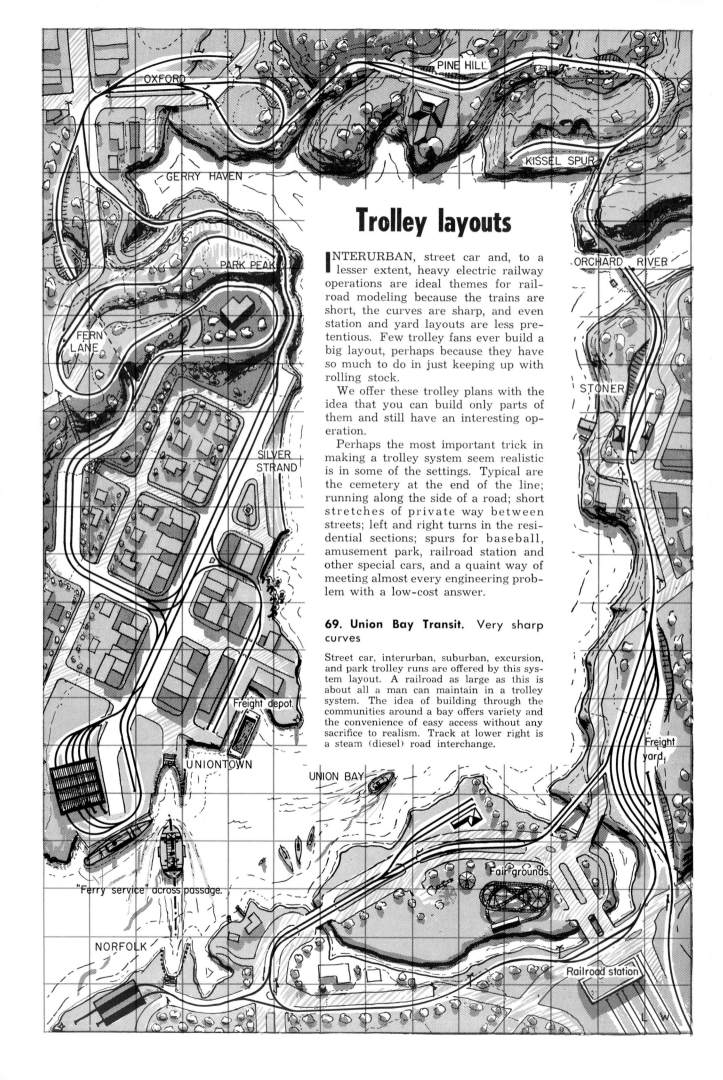

Trolley layouts

INTERURBAN, street car and, to a lesser extent, heavy electric railway operations are ideal themes for railroad modeling because the trains are short, the curves are sharp, and even station and yard layouts are less pretentious. Few trolley fans ever build a big layout, perhaps because they have so much to do in just keeping up with rolling stock.

We offer these trolley plans with the idea that you can build only parts of them and still have an interesting operation.

Perhaps the most important trick in making a trolley system seem realistic is in some of the settings. Typical are the cemetery at the end of the line; running along the side of a road; short stretches of private way between streets; left and right turns in the residential sections; spurs for baseball, amusement park, railroad station and other special cars, and a quaint way of meeting almost every engineering problem with a low-cost answer.

69. Union Bay Transit. Very sharp curves

Street car, interurban, suburban, excursion, and park trolley runs are offered by this system layout. A railroad as large as this is about all a man can maintain in a trolley system. The idea of building through the communities around a bay offers variety and the convenience of easy access without any sacrifice to realism. Track at lower right is a steam (diesel) road interchange.

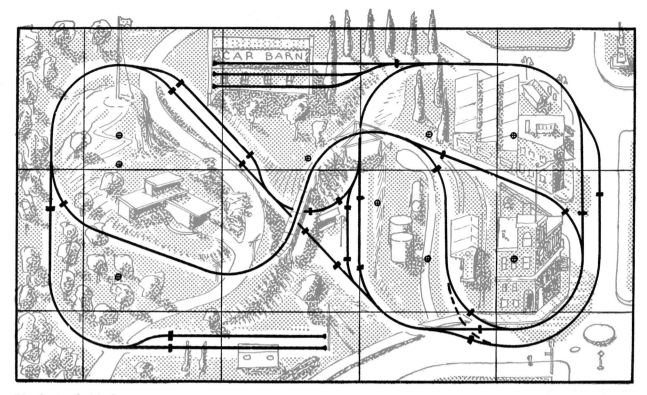

70. Springfield Electric Lines. Very sharp curves

At the two overpasses the upper track should be 4" above the lower (HO) and the grades connecting the upper and lower level should be uniform.

Ruled lines across plan are:

Plan 69	Plans 70, 71
6" apart in N	12" apart in N
9" apart in TT	18" apart in TT
12" apart in HO	24" apart in HO
18" apart in S	36" apart in S
24" apart in O	48" apart in O

See page 70 for more data.

71. Hillsboro Traction Co. Very sharp

This electric railroad could be a real gem with the trolley wire well strung and the scenery nicely done. Putting the streets at an angle increases the apparent size of the space.

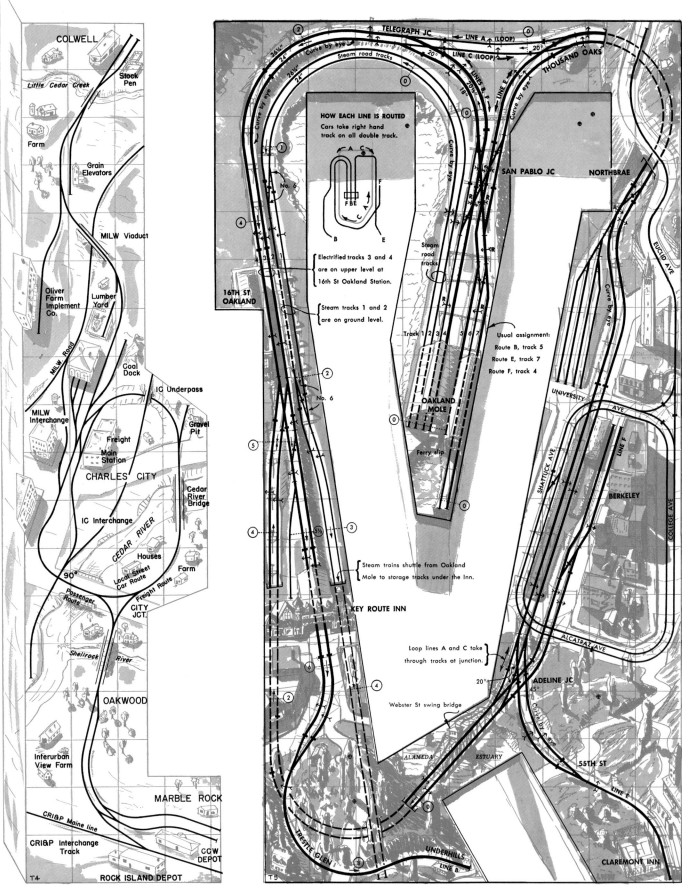

72. Charles City Western RR. Very sharp curves

Good industries along the line, plus interchange connections with three large railroads, have kept the real CCW going for years. Our plan is similar to the real track routes.

73. Golden Key Route. Sharp curves

The "East Bay" cities along San Francisco Bay used to have a wonderful suburban service operated by competing companies. Much of the track was at street level and the automobile hampered the running of trains. Little of this is left today, but I've tried to recapture highlights in this composite system. The Berkeley street car has 7½" curves.

Larger shelf railroads

for long narrow spaces

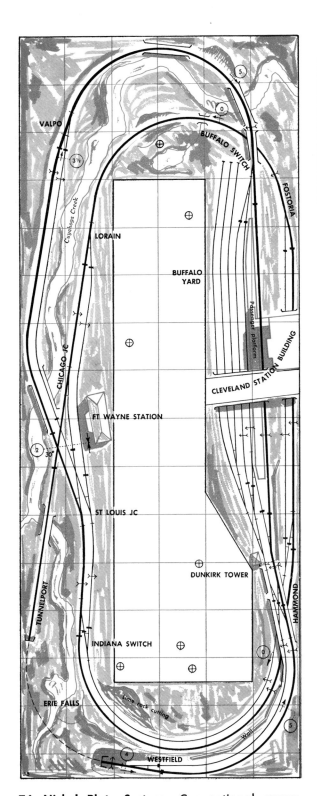

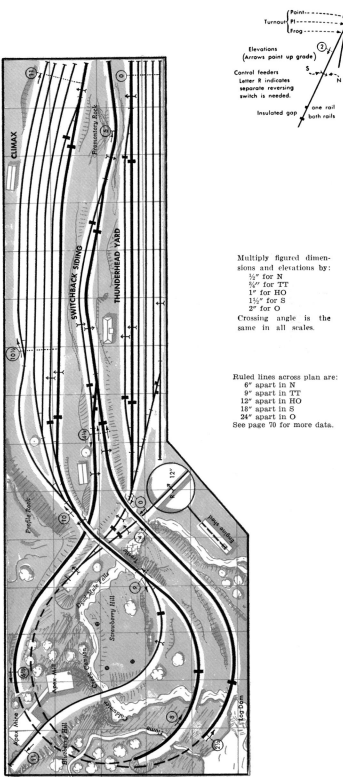

Main route - - - -
Other track - - - -
Hidden track · · · · · · ·
Optional route - - - - -

Center of important curve ●

Turnout Point - - - -
Pt - - - -
Frog - - - -

Elevations (Arrows point up grade)

Control feeders Letter R indicates separate reversing switch is needed.

Insulated gap   one rail   both rails

Multiply figured dimensions and elevations by:
½" for N
¾" for TT
1" for HO
1½" for S
2" for O
Crossing angle is the same in all scales.

Ruled lines across plan are:
6" apart in N
9" apart in TT
12" apart in HO
18" apart in S
24" apart in O
See page 70 for more data.

74. Nickel Plate System. Conventional curves

This two-lap oval should be easy to build and maintain. It can be improved by adding industrial switching spurs.

75. Thunderhead & Climax RR. Conventional curves

Here's another version of the switchback that works its way up a mountainside. This one provides rather large yards.

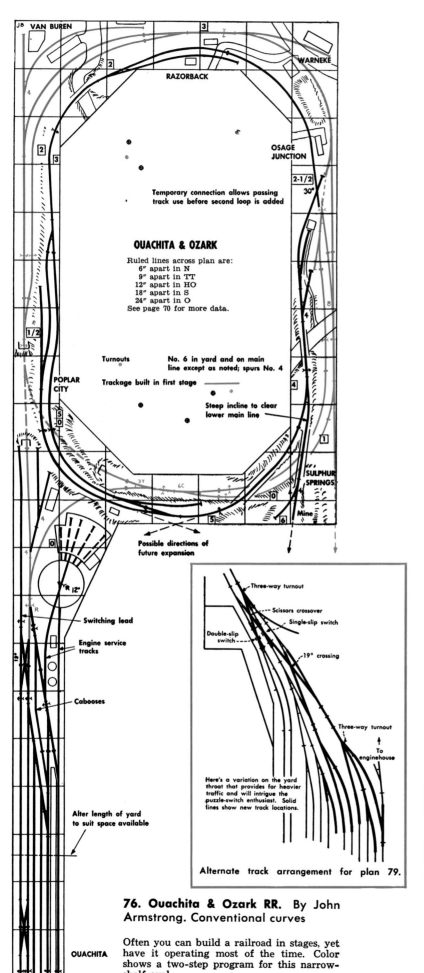

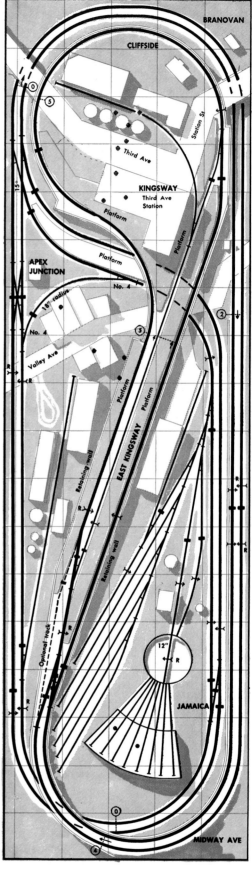

76. Ouachita & Ozark RR. By John Armstrong. Conventional curves

Often you can build a railroad in stages, yet have it operating most of the time. Color shows a two-step program for this narrow-shelf oval.

77. Jamaica & Kingsway Short Line. Conventional curves with one sharp curve in the wye

This railroad is based on a very popular plan originally planned by Lt. Comdr. Ralph Butterfield for use in a single-car garage space.

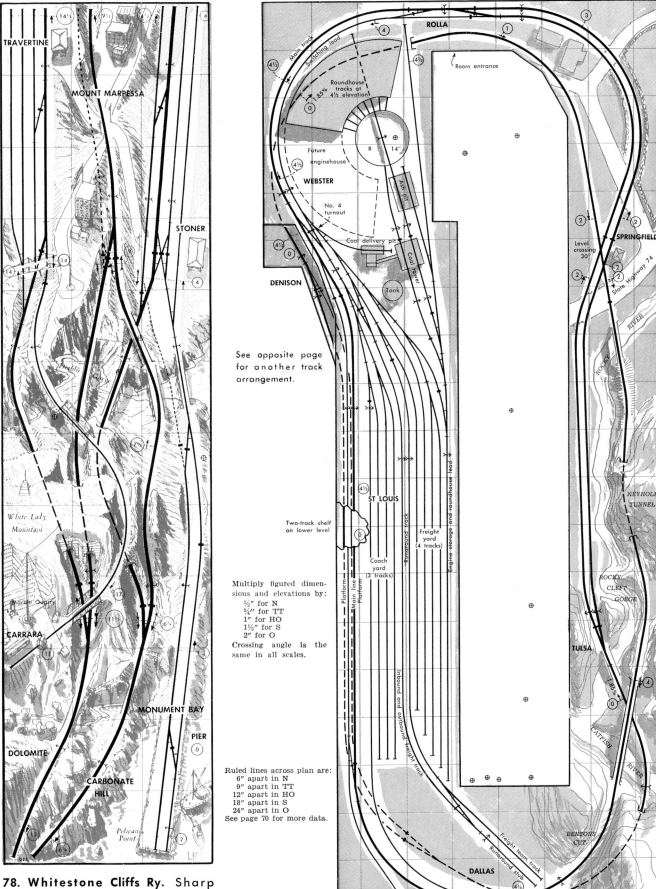

78. Whitestone Cliffs Ry. Sharp curves

This one handles marble from a hilltop quarry to the pier. Future track at Mount Marpessa will allow up trains and down trains to pass. Note that this plan is drawn to a different scale.

See opposite page for another track arrangement.

Multiply figured dimensions and elevations by:
½″ for N
¾″ for TT
1″ for HO
1½″ for S
2″ for O
Crossing angle is the same in all scales.

Ruled lines across plan are:
6″ apart in N
9″ apart in TT
12″ apart in HO
18″ apart in S
24″ apart in O
See page 70 for more data.

79. Frisco Lines. Broad curves

This railroad makes more of the yard than most plans do. Even then it has plenty of room for industries, scenery, and space for the operator. Track-minded men may prefer the variation on page 46.

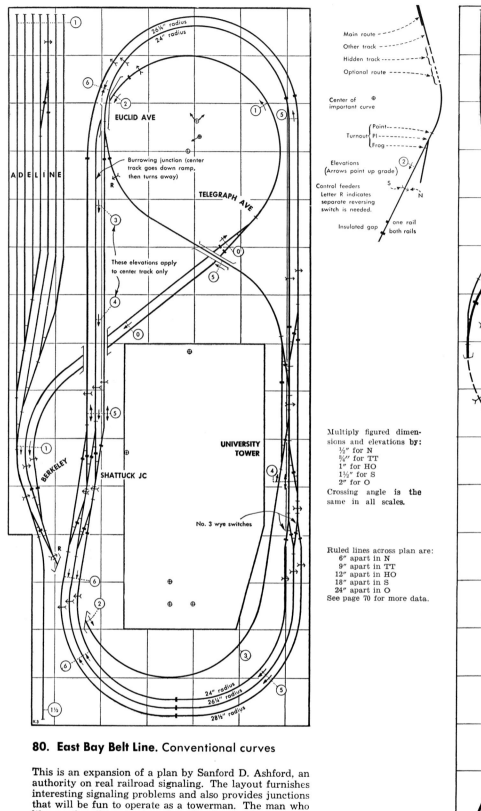

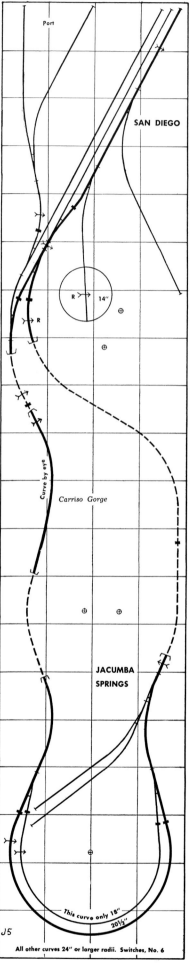

80. East Bay Belt Line. Conventional curves

This is an expansion of a plan by Sanford D. Ashford, an authority on real railroad signaling. The layout furnishes interesting signaling problems and also provides junctions that will be fun to operate as a towerman. The man who likes railroadlike trackwork will also be happy with this type of model railroad.

81. San Diego & Arizona Eastern RR. Conventional curves with an exception

You'll have to make the table wider than four feet if you want to use 24″ and 26¼″ radii curves at Jacumba. Otherwise this railroad can handle any locomotive.

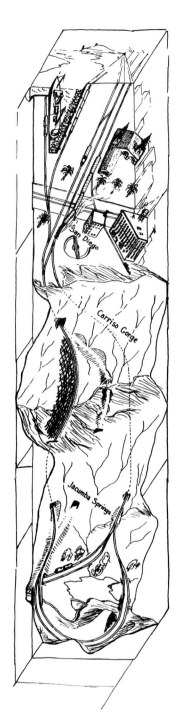

81. SD&AE. See opposite page

Railroads for a single garage

82. Toledo & Southern Michigan RR.
Conventional curves

The facilities of this road are so spread out that it could be used nicely for either club or home. Space along right side must be an aisle for operating.

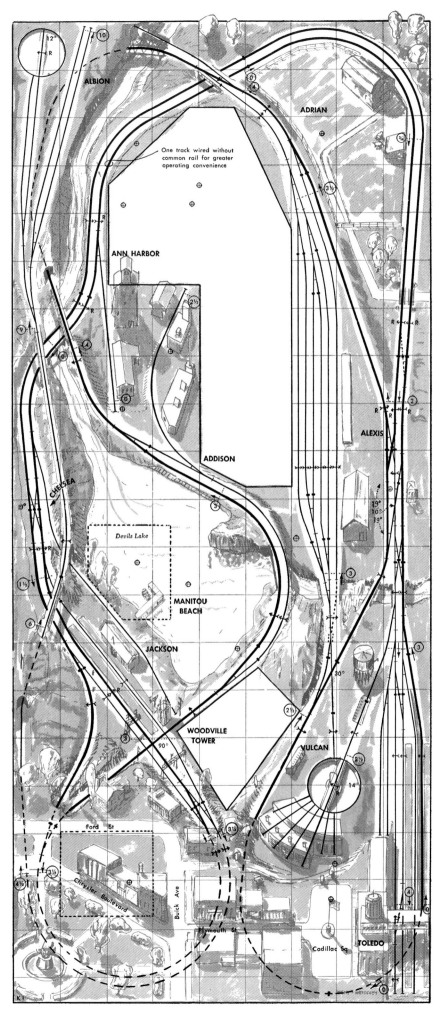

One track wired without common rail for greater operating convenience

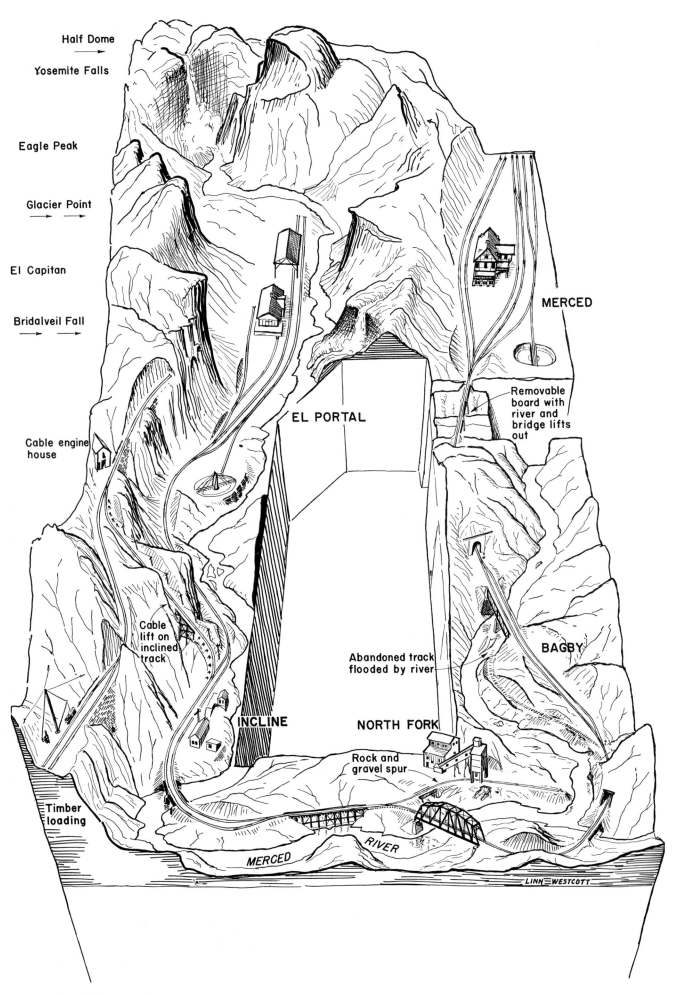

Half Dome

Yosemite Falls

Eagle Peak

Glacier Point

El Capitan

Bridalveil Fall

Cable engine house

MERCED

Removable board with river and bridge lifts out

EL PORTAL

Cable lift on inclined track

Abandoned track flooded by river

BAGBY

INCLINE

NORTH FORK

Rock and gravel spur

Timber loading

MERCED   RIVER

LINN WESTCOTT

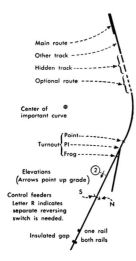

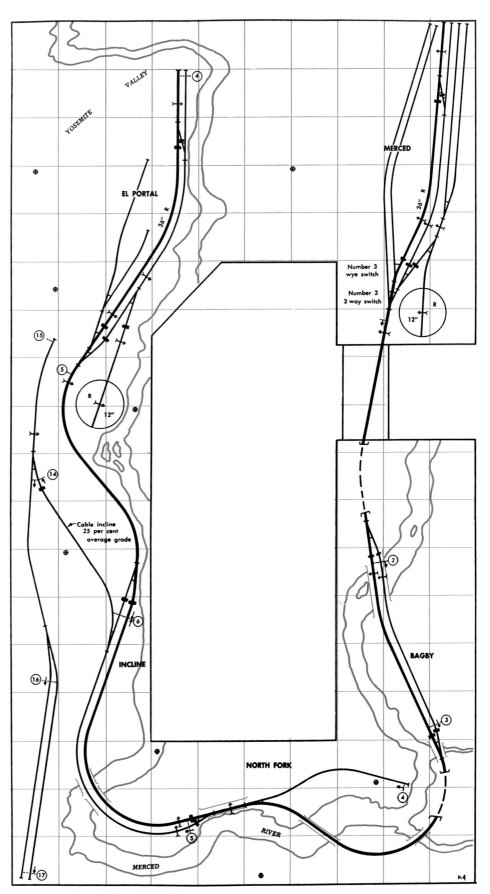

Multiply figured dimensions
and elevations by:
½″ for N
¾″ for TT
1″ for HO
1½″ for S
2″ for O

Ruled lines across plan are:
6″ apart in N
9″ apart in TT
12″ apart in HO
18″ apart in S
24″ apart in O
See page 70 for more data.

83. Yosemite Valley RR. Sharp curves

Once upon a time you could ride to the portals of wonderful Yosemite National Park through a glorious canyon along Merced River in the luxury of a fine observation car. One of the features along the line was an incline where timber was lowered to mainline level on flat cars held back by a cable. The cars had a bulkhead built at the lower end to keep the logs from sliding. The cable was at the side rather than between the rails. In Merced Yard, three-way and wye switches save space.

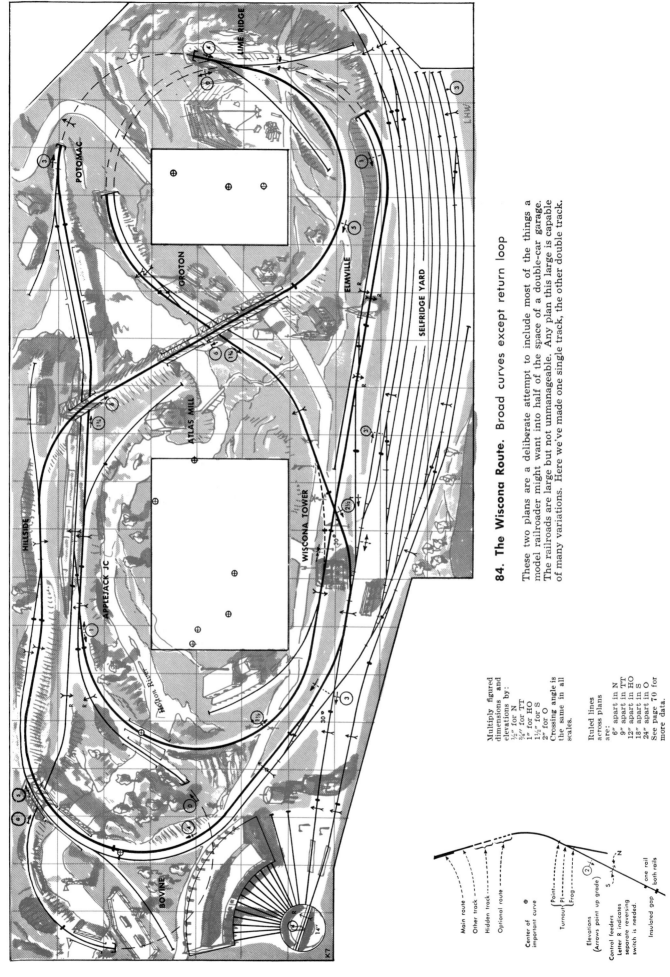

84. The Wiscona Route. Broad curves except return loop

These two plans are a deliberate attempt to include most of the things a model railroader might want into half of the space of a double-car garage. The railroads are large but not unmanageable. Any plan this large is capable of many variations. Here we've made one single track, the other double track.

Multiply figured dimensions and elevations by:
½″ for N
¾″ for TT
1″ for HO
1½″ for S
2″ for O
Crossing angle is the same in all scales.

Ruled lines across plans are:
6″ apart in N
9″ apart in TT
12″ apart in HO
18″ apart in S
24″ apart in O
See page 70 for more data.

Main route ––––––
Other track - - - - -
Hidden track - - - - -
Optional route · · · · · ·

Center of ⊕
important curve

Turnout { Point
          Pl
          Frog }

Elevations
(Arrows point up grade)

Control feeders
Letter R indicates
separate reversing
switch is needed.   S

Insulated gap   one rail
                 both rails   N

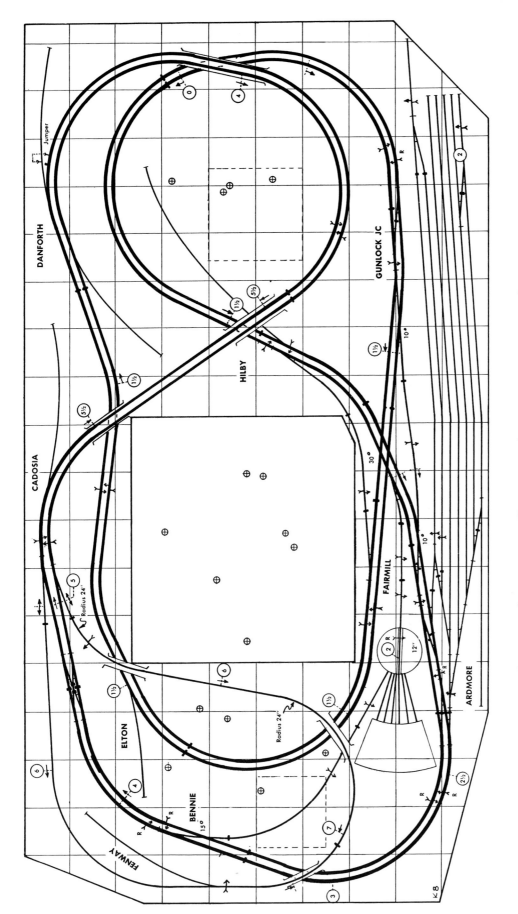

85. Ardmore, Cadosia & Fairmill RR. Broad curves except return loop

This two-track version changes the operation some because trains going in opposite directions need not make meets. Frequently we have named the stations on a railroad in alphabetical order. This is a help when you have visitors who want to help operate, but don't yet know your railroad thoroughly. A few other plans in this book are named in this way.

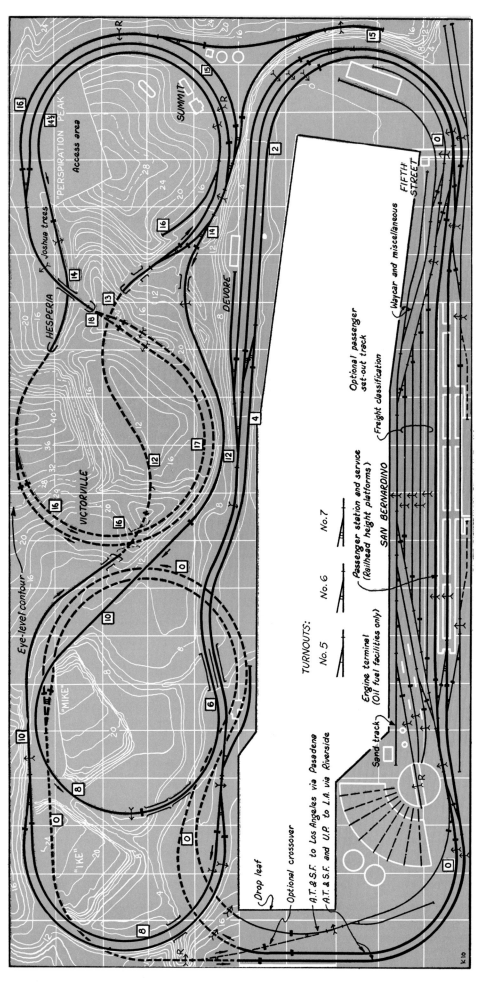

TURNOUTS:

No. 5   No. 6   No. 7

86. Cajon Pass, Salt Lake & Santa Fe RR. By John
Armstrong. Conventional curves

Much of the transcontinental traffic to Los Angeles winds
its way down steep Cajon Pass to San Bernardino. Both
Santa Fe and Union Pacific share the track. Armstrong's
plan features the rock outcroppings, the divided main
line, and the interesting station at the bottom of the grade.
Hardly any plan could be better to display your cars and
locomotives.

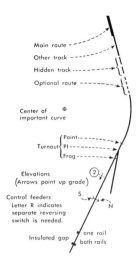

Main route
Other track
Hidden track
Optional route

Center of important curve

Turnout { Point
          Pl
          Frog

Elevations
(Arrows point up grade)

Control feeders
Letter R indicates separate reversing switch is needed.

Insulated gap
one rail
both rails

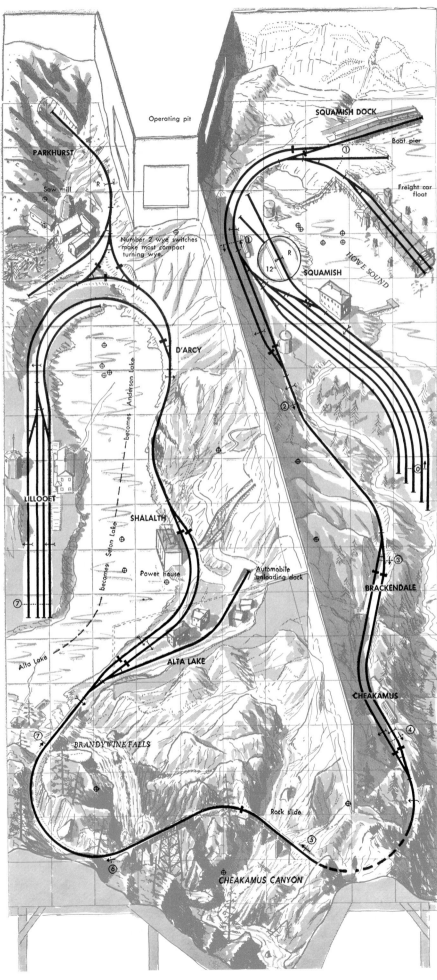

PARKHURST

Saw mill

Operating pit

SQUAMISH DOCK

Boat pier

Freight car float

Number 2 wye switches make most compact turning wye

SQUAMISH

HOWE SOUND

12"

D'ARCY

becomes Anderson Lake

LILLOOET

SHALALTH

becomes Seton Lake

Power house

Automobile unloading dock

BRACKENDALE

Alta Lake

ALTA LAKE

CHEAKAMUS

BRANDYWINE FALLS

Rock slide

CHEAKAMUS CANYON

87. Pacific Great Eastern RR. Sharp curves

Only recently has the southern end (upper right) of the real PGE been extended to reach the city of Vancouver, B.C. We show the line as it used to be, getting passengers by boat and freight cars by car float. The parts on each side of the central back-drop could be turned in other directions to make an L or else an around-the-wall type of plan.

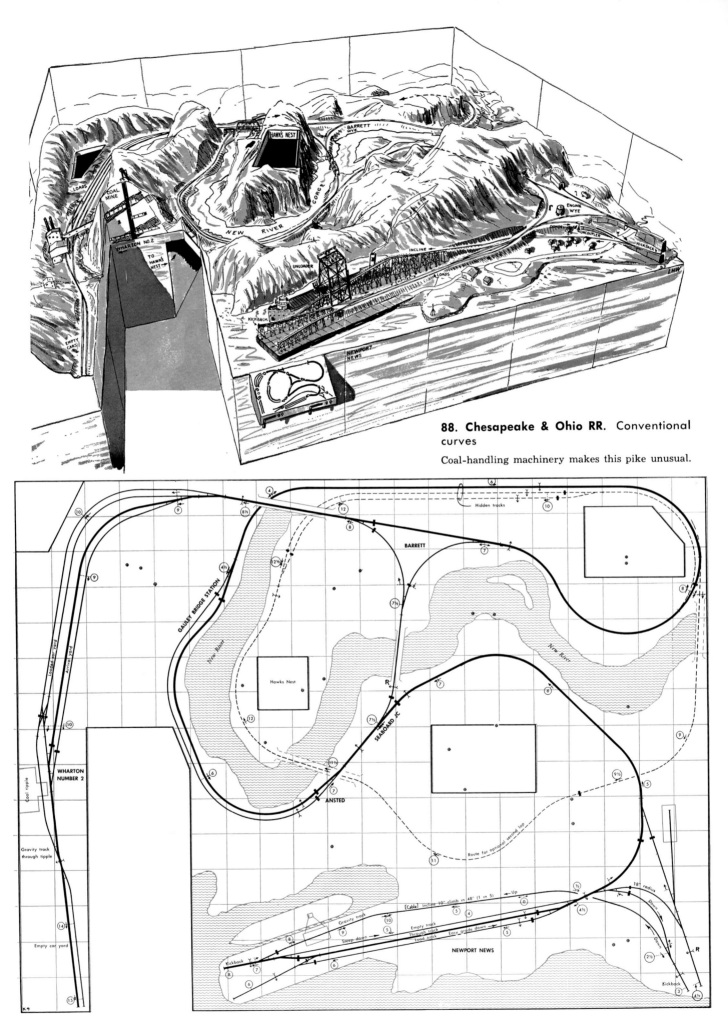

88. Chesapeake & Ohio RR. Conventional curves

Coal-handling machinery makes this pike unusual.

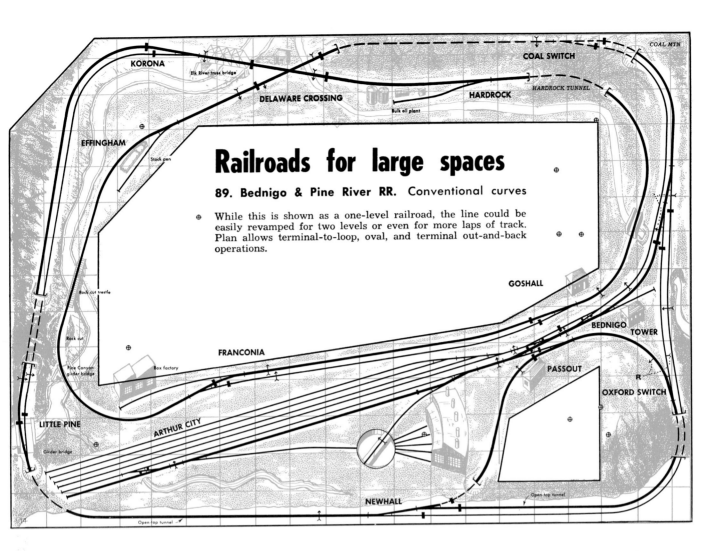

Railroads for large spaces

89. Bednigo & Pine River RR. Conventional curves

⊕ While this is shown as a one-level railroad, the line could be easily revamped for two levels or even for more laps of track. Plan allows terminal-to-loop, oval, and terminal out-and-back operations.

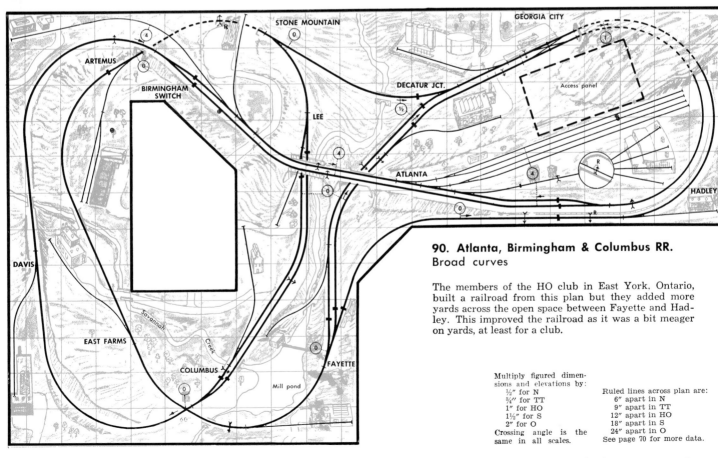

90. Atlanta, Birmingham & Columbus RR.
Broad curves

The members of the HO club in East York, Ontario, built a railroad from this plan but they added more yards across the open space between Fayette and Hadley. This improved the railroad as it was a bit meager on yards, at least for a club.

Multiply figured dimensions and elevations by:
½″ for N
¾″ for TT
1″ for HO
1½″ for S
2″ for O
Crossing angle is the same in all scales.

Ruled lines across plan are:
6″ apart in N
9″ apart in TT
12″ apart in HO
18″ apart in S
24″ apart in O
See page 70 for more data.

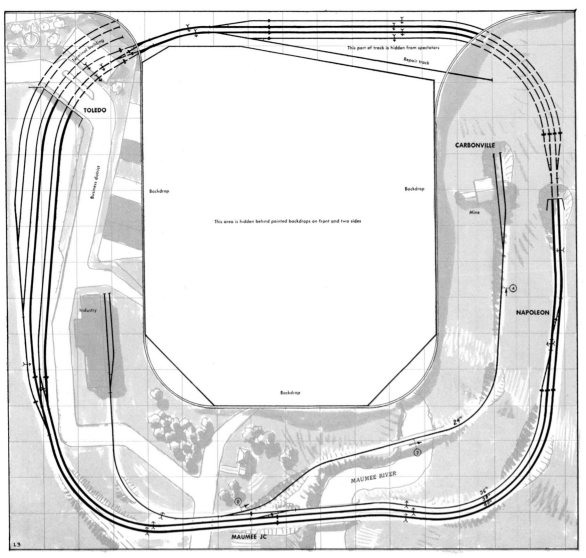

TOLEDO

Terminal building

Business district

Backdrop

Backdrop

This area is hidden behind painted backdrops on front and two sides

This part of track is hidden from spectators

Repair track

CARBONVILLE

Mine

NAPOLEON

Industry

Backdrop

24"

2

MAUMEE RIVER

36"
34"
0°

0

L3

MAUMEE JC

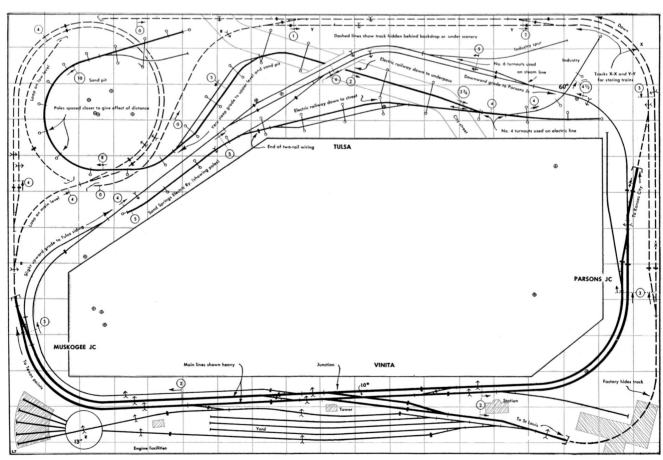

4

0

R
Y

1

Y

Dashed lines show track hidden behind backdrop or under scenery

Y

2

Down

X

10

Sand pit

Poles spaced closer to give effect of distance

Loop on low level

5

5

5

6

2

Industry spur

Electric railway down to underpass

5

No. 6 turnouts used on steam line

Downward grade to Parsons Jc

Industry

Tracks X-X and Y-Y for storing trains

X

Very steep grade to upper level and sand pit

Electric railway down to street

0

60°

3¾

4½

4

3

8

5

End of two-rail wiring

TULSA

City street

4

No. 4 turnouts used on electric line

Loop on main level

4

0

4

Sand Springs Electric Ry. (showing poles)

Slight upward grade to Tulsa siding

5

R

To Kansas City

PARSONS JC

3

3

MUSKOGEE JC

To Texas points

VINITA

Main lines shown heavy

Junction

2

10°

Station

2

Factory hides track

Tower

To St Louis

Yard

13" R

Engine facilities

L7

91. Opposite page. **Toledo & Indiana RR.** Display railroad with broad curves

This railroad was planned for a museum with the special problems of operation and maintenance kept in mind. The central area is a hidden repair shop. At the upper right are holding tracks so alternate trains can be operated. The branch can be operated by a switcher shunting from mine to industry without reaching the mainline tracks.

Multiply figured dimensions and elevations by:
½″ for N
¾″ for TT
1″ for HO
1½″ for S
2″ for O
Crossing angle is the same in all scales.

Main route ------
Other track ------
Hidden track ------
Optional route ------

Center of ⊕
important curve

Turnout { Point ------
PI ------
Frog ------

Elevations
(Arrows point up grade)

Control feeders
Letter R indicates
separate reversing
switch is needed.

Insulated gap   one rail
both rails

92. Opposite page. **Missouri-Kansas-Texas System.** Conventional curves

This is really two railroads. The steam-diesel system with a big yard and hidden loops and holding tracks, as well as one line that stays in sight around the room, is one system. Connecting to it at Tulsa is an electric industrial line. (Maybe it takes passengers too.) This winds down from a gravel pit to the main street. It must switch back twice to reach the interchange with the big railroad.

Ruled lines across plan are:
6″ apart in N
9″ apart in TT
12″ apart in HO
18″ apart in S
24″ apart in O
See page 70 for more data.

LEBANON
HARTSVILLE
HERMITAGE
NASHVILLE
CARTHAGE
COOKEVILLE
TENNESSEE RIVER
MONTEREY
DONELSON
OLD HICKORY
MADISON
LIVINGSTON
WILDER

93. Tennessee Eastern Ry. Broad curves

This railroad was designed for the Children's Museum in Nashville, Tenn., and the O gauge club of Nashville built and operate it.

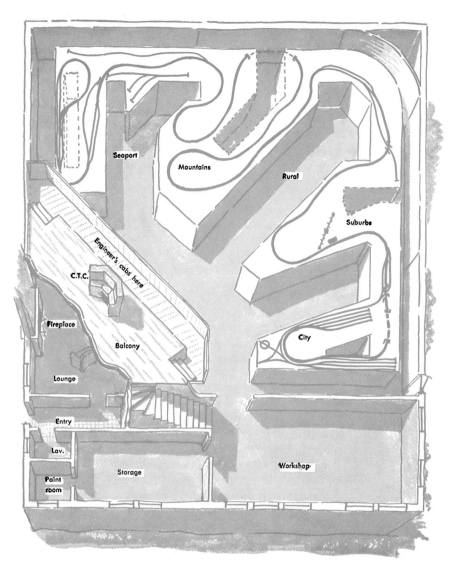

Estate-size railroad

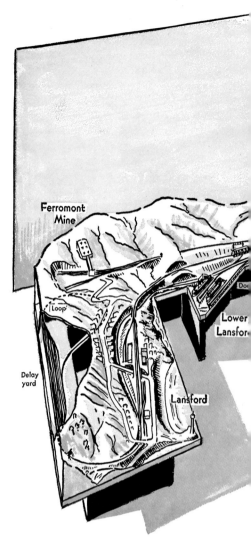

If I had a million

What kind of a railroad would you build if given unlimited funds?

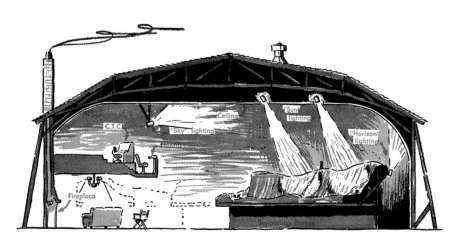

This section through the railroad room shows the three kinds of lighting that combine to make a sun-and-clouds effect. The ceiling is white so that colors other than blue can be played on the sky.

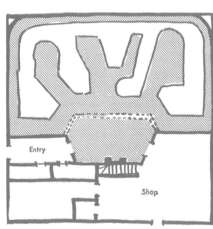

Club-size railroad

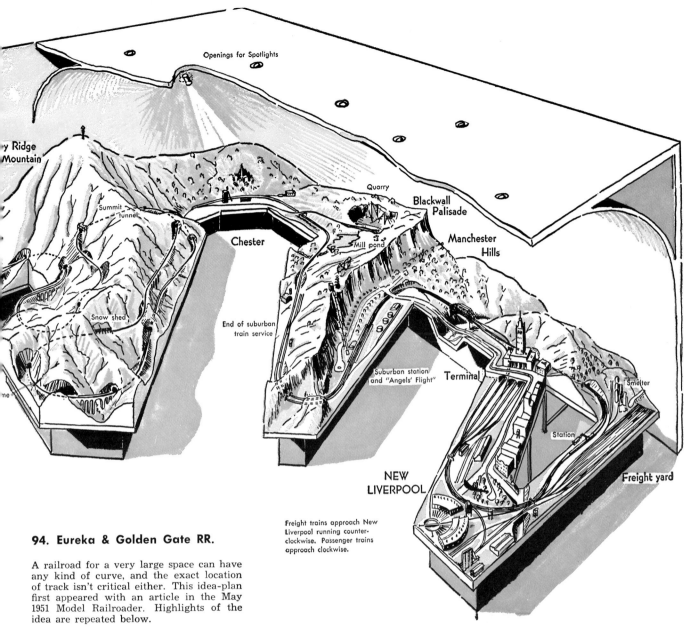

Openings for Spotlights

y Ridge
Mountain

Summit
Tunnel

Snow shed

Quarry

Blackwall
Palisade

Chester

Mill pond

Manchester
Hills

End of suburban
train service

Suburban station
and "Angels' Flight"

Terminal

Smelter

Station

NEW
LIVERPOOL

Freight yard

94. Eureka & Golden Gate RR.

A railroad for a very large space can have
any kind of curve, and the exact location
of track isn't critical either. This idea-plan
first appeared with an article in the May
1951 Model Railroader. Highlights of the
idea are repeated below.

Freight trains approach New
Liverpool running counterclockwise. Passenger trains
approach clockwise.

WHEN money and space are no
problem in building a railroad,
there are still practical limitations
such as determining just what size it
will be and the method of planning it.
This railroad isn't impossibly big, at
least for a club, for as this is written a
version of it is well under way at the
HO club in the B&O station at Wheel-
ing, W. Va.

A super railroad should be big
enough to keep a man busy at his
hobby of building, operating and re-
building. It shouldn't be so large,
however, that maintenance takes up
more time than construction. Here
are some of the ideas incorporated
into this plan:

The building is designed specifically
to house the railroad. A ground floor
entrance, workshop, storage space and
lounging area are provided, con-

venient to the layout. A balcony provides bird's eye viewing and an operating position for mainline track
running. Switching and way freights
are handled while walking alongside
the trains.

The aisles are arranged radially so
you can either stand at one point and
see all of the railroad, or you can walk
into one bay to get a realistic view
of just one scene.

A room 60 x 65 feet is best for this
railroad in HO, but similar arrangements can be worked into spaces of 50
feet, or perhaps less. The railroad
room needs no windows; in fact, it
shouldn't have them, but good dust-
proof ventilation or air conditioning is
desirable. Lighting consists of even
"sky light" reflected from a curved
false ceiling. Holes through the ceiling allow yellowish spot lights to send

beams of "sunlight" down as though
from openings between clouds. All
spotlights are pointed at the same
downward angle and their beams do
not overlap.

The railroad itself must be a plan
that looks like a possible, if not entirely probable, scene in any close-up
view. Loop-to-loop operation is almost essential unless there's going to
be plenty of manpower available to
switch trains in the terminals. Natu-
rally, switching is wanted, but it's
hard to keep the main line busy if all
trains must be turned in a yard. The
loops let many trains turn easily.

Track doesn't ever return into the
same scene twice except to climb to
the summit.

Angels' Fleight is a funicular (cable
railroad) to a pagoda and amusement
park atop Blackwall Palisade.

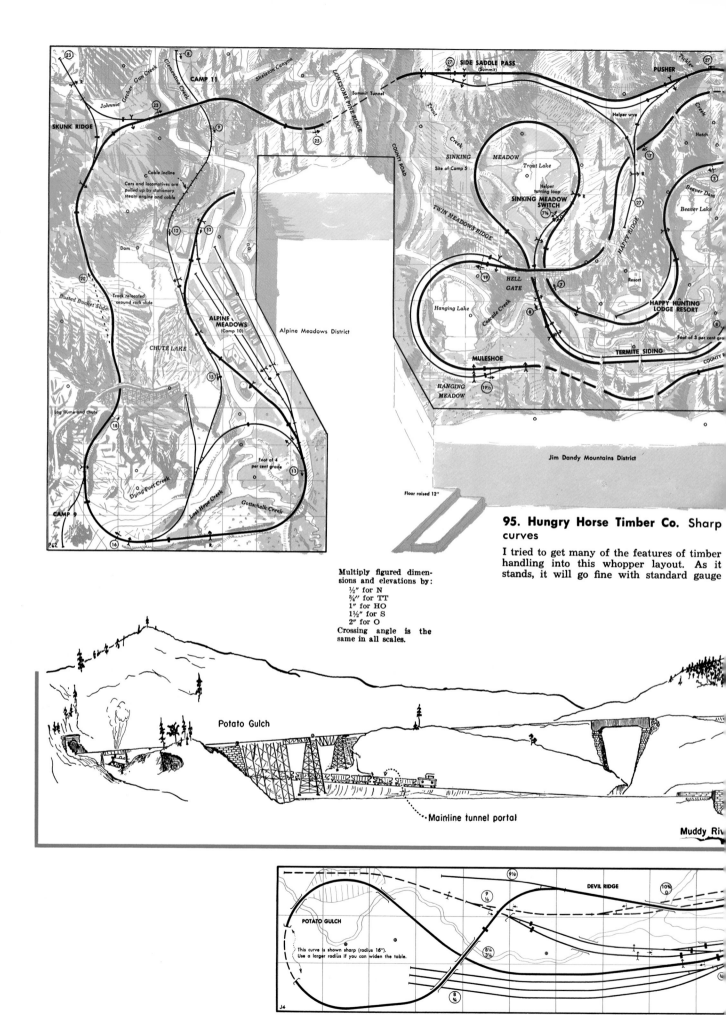

Multiply figured dimensions and elevations by:
½" for N
¾" for TT
1" for HO
1½" for S
2" for O
Crossing angle is the same in all scales.

95. Hungry Horse Timber Co. Sharp curves

I tried to get many of the features of timber handling into this whopper layout. As it stands, it will go fine with standard gauge

Potato Gulch

Mainline tunnel portal

Muddy Riv

This curve is shown sharp (radius 16"). Use a larger radius if you can widen the table.

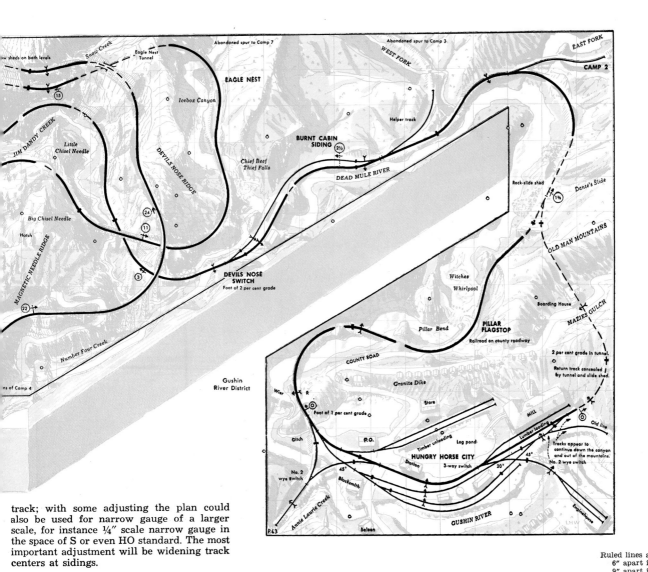

Abandoned spur to Camp 7
Abandoned spur to Camp 3
EAST FORK
WEST FORK
CAMP 2
sheds on both levels
Snow Creek
Eagle Nest Tunnel
EAGLE NEST
Icebox Canyon
(15)
JIM DANDY CREEK
Little Chisel Needle
DEVILS NOSE RIDGE
Chief Beef Thief Falls
BURNT CABIN SIDING (2½)
Helper track
DEAD MULE RIVER
Rock-slide shed
Dante's Slide
(1¾)
(24)
Big Chisel Needle
OLD MAN MOUNTAINS
(11)
Hatch
MAGNETIC NEEDLE RIDGE
(3)
DEVILS NOSE SWITCH
Foot of 2 per cent grade
Witches Whirlpool
Boarding House
MAZIES GULCH
(22)
Number Four Creek
Pillar Bend
PILLAR FLAGSTOP
Railroad on county roadway
2 per cent grade in tunnel
Return track concealed by tunnel and slide shed.
ns of Camp 4
Gushin River District
COUNTY ROAD
Granite Dike
Store
MILL
Old line
Weir
R
Foot of 1 per cent grade
Lumber loading
Tracks appear to continue down the canyon and out of the mountains. No. 2 wye switch
Ditch
P.O.
Timber unloading
Log pond
45°
No. 2 wye switch
HUNGRY HORSE CITY
Station
3-way switch
20°
45°
Blacksmith
Enginehouse
Annie Laurie Creek
Saloon
GUSHIN RIVER
P.63
L.H.W.

track; with some adjusting the plan could also be used for narrow gauge of a larger scale, for instance ¼″ scale narrow gauge in the space of S or even HO standard. The most important adjustment will be widening track centers at sidings.

Ruled lines across plan are:
6″ apart in N
9″ apart in TT
12″ apart in HO
18″ apart in S
24″ apart in O
See page 70 for more data.

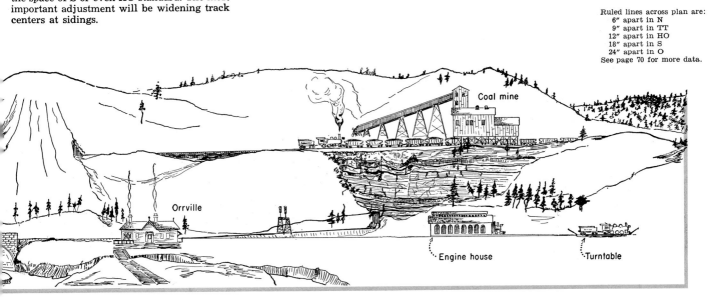

Coal mine
Orrville
Engine house
Turntable

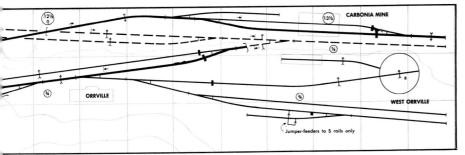

12½
CARBONIA MINE
13½
½
ORRVILLE
¾
¾
WEST ORRVILLE
R
Jumper-feeders to S rails only

96. Orrville Mining RR. Sharp curves

Hidden tracks allow mainline trains to serve Orrville from both directions. Two mainline trains can be used, one headed each way. After leaving Orrville in either direction, they back into their storage sidings inside the mountain. Of course, the important operation here is the branch line to the mine.

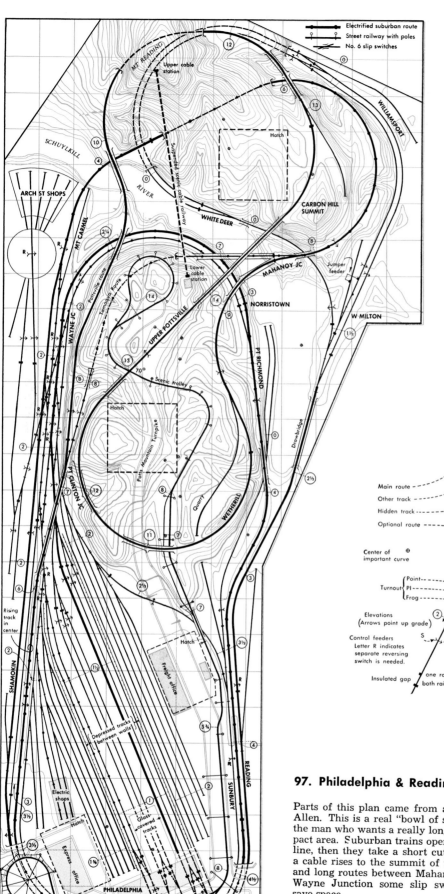

Legend (top of map):
- ●──●──● Electrified suburban route
- Street railway with poles
- No. 6 slip switches

Key (right side of page):
- Main route - - - -
- Other track - - - -
- Hidden track - - - - -
- Optional route - - - - -

Center of ⊕ important curve

Turnout { Point - - - - / PI - - - - / Frog - - - - }

Elevations (Arrows point up grade)

Control feeders
Letter R indicates separate reversing switch is needed.

Insulated gap { one rail / both rails }

97. Philadelphia & Reading System. Broad curves

Parts of this plan came from another railroad that I designed for George Allen. This is a real "bowl of spaghetti" type of plan and should appeal to the man who wants a really long main line and interesting routing in a compact area. Suburban trains operate from overhead catenary over part of the line, then they take a short cut back to the terminal. A suspended car on a cable rises to the summit of the mountain on the hour. Notice the short and long routes between Mahanoy Junction and Port Clinton Junction. At Wayne Junction some slip switches are needed both for looks and to save space.

Multiply figured dimensions and elevations by:
- ½″ for N
- ¾″ for TT
- 1″ for HO
- 1½″ for S
- 2″ for O

Crossing angle is the same in all scales.

Ruled lines across plan are:
- 6″ apart in N
- 9″ apart in TT
- 12″ apart in HO
- 18″ apart in S
- 24″ apart in O

See page 70 for more data.

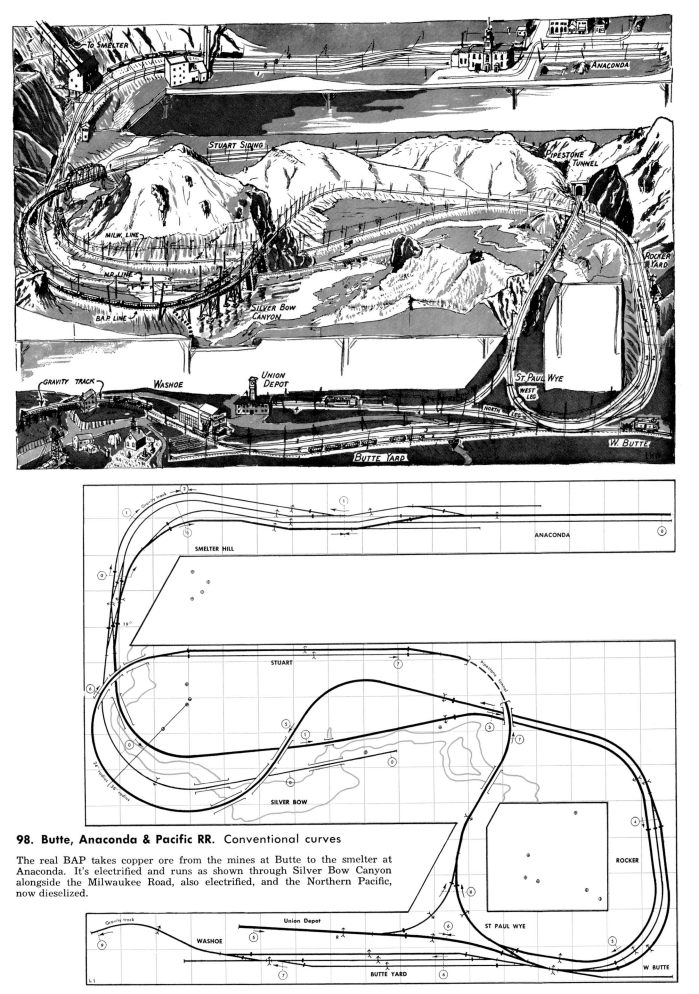

98. Butte, Anaconda & Pacific RR. Conventional curves

The real BAP takes copper ore from the mines at Butte to the smelter at Anaconda. It's electrified and runs as shown through Silver Bow Canyon alongside the Milwaukee Road, also electrified, and the Northern Pacific, now dieselized.

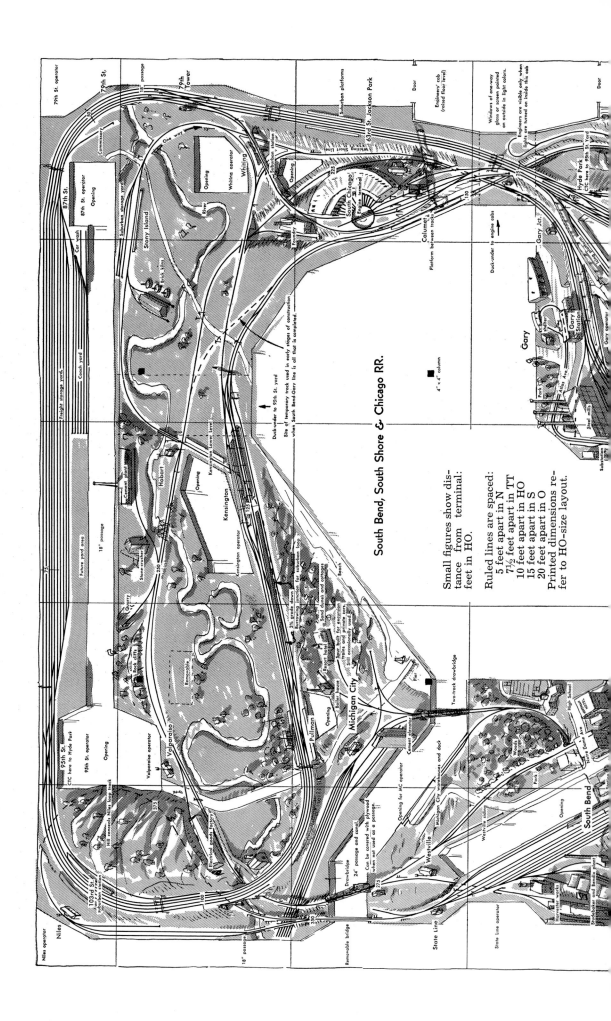

South Bend, South Shore & Chicago RR.

Small figures show distance from terminal: feet in HO.

Ruled lines are spaced:
5 feet apart in N
7½ feet apart in TT
10 feet apart in HO
15 feet apart in S
20 feet apart in O
Printed dimensions refer to HO-size layout.

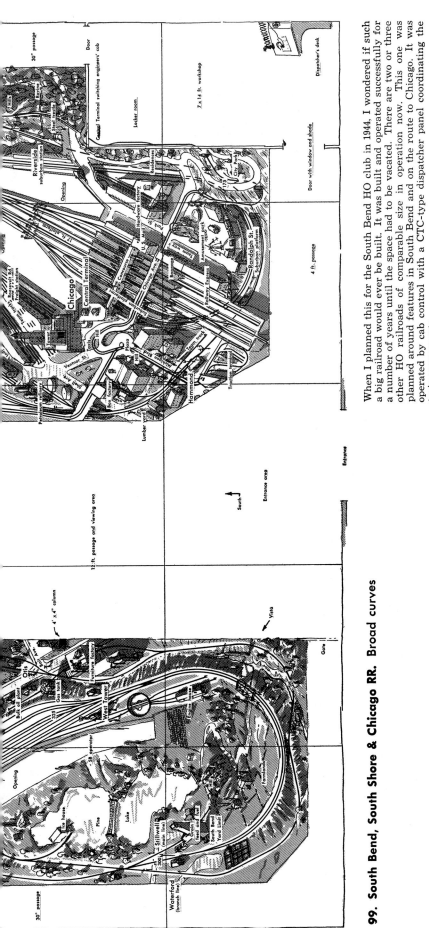

99. South Bend, South Shore & Chicago RR. Broad curves

When I planned this for the South Bend HO club in 1944, I wondered if such a big railroad would ever be built. It was built and operated successfully for a number of years until the space had to be vacated. There are two or three other HO railroads of comparable size in operation now. This one was planned around features in South Bend and on the route to Chicago. It was operated by cab control with a CTC-type dispatcher panel coordinating the train movements.

Continued from page 8

interfere with operations, so be sure you know what you are doing.

How about feeders?

Move them to any convenient place along the very same rail, but not beyond any gaps in the rails.

What do I do when the letter R appears near track feeders?

Eventually you'll want to build a control panel such as the dual-throttle type on page 57 of the book *How to Wire Your Model Railroad*, but at first you can get by with only one extra reversing switch of the double-pole double-throw type.

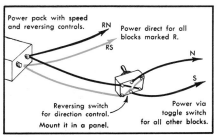

Connect all mainline tracks through this switch. Connect R feeders direct to your regular controls, bypassing the new direction-control switch.

How are crossings wired?

Our plans are wired with the assumption that all crossings have jumpered wiring. This is the way most, if not all, commercial crossings are made.

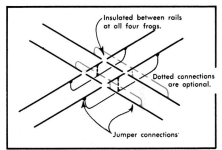

How about scissors or double crossovers?

Most commercially made crossovers don't have enough gaps for proper two-train operation. There should be no way for electricity to get from one approach of the crossover to any other. Usually you must cut your own gaps at XX in addition to those ready made.

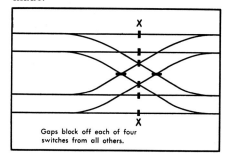

Continued from page 37

You certainly want to reach the switches of a yard from a convenient aisle. All small plans present this problem, and you should keep it in mind when looking for a suitable one. Larger plans usually provide operating aisles within the table space.

If one side of the railroad must be tight against a wall, either choose a side that has few if any switches, or else provide 18"-square hatches where you can pop up through the scenery to get at them.

If your room is large enough, try to provide an 18" aisle behind all parts of the railroad and a 36" or wider aisle wherever visitors will want to go; 24" is enough for one-man control spaces.

Do many of these plans seem too complicated?

We've put a lot of detail into our plans to help you with construction. This makes them look much more complex than if you saw just the track lines alone. But if the plans for your size of space still have more in them than you want, choose a plan for a smaller space and build it instead. You can easily blow any plan up to a larger size by methods explained on page 5.

Don't overlook the idea of building plans as simple as those on page 2 into spaces two or more times as big.

100. Ohio Central System. Conventional curves

This plan is quite adaptable to variations both in scenic treatment and in the routing of main lines. The terminal is easily accessible. Black Hand Gorge is a real place, near Newark, Ohio, where an old canal towpath in ruins skirts the river. The nearby tunnel was for an interurban line, but I've used it for the steam-diesel road instead.

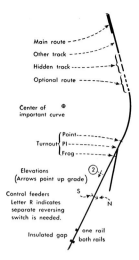

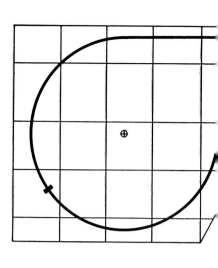

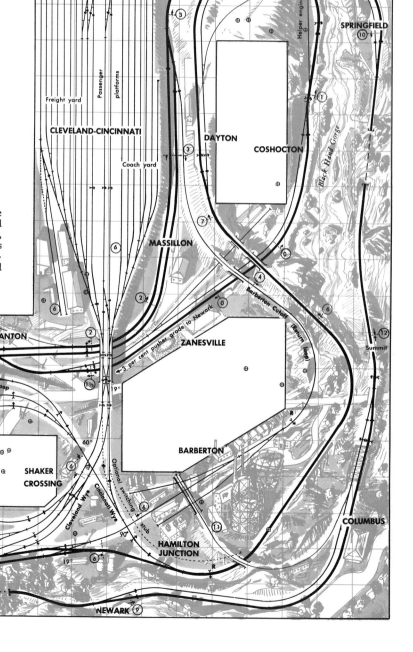

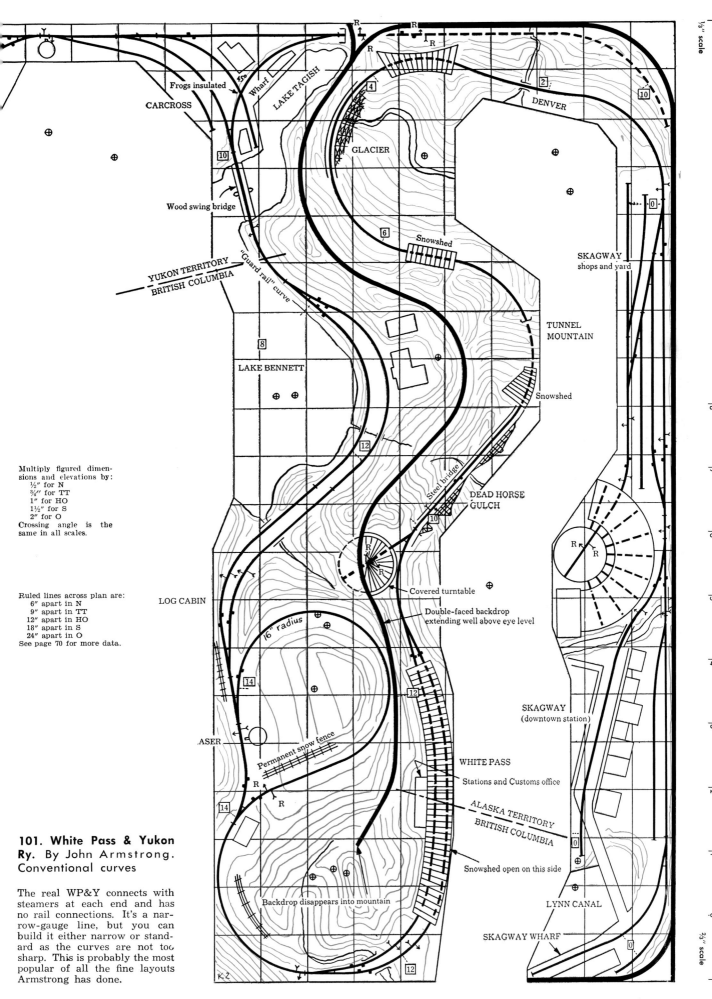

Frogs insulated

Wharf

LAKE TAGISH

CARCROSS

GLACIER

Wood swing bridge

YUKON TERRITORY
BRITISH COLUMBIA

"Guard rail" curve

LAKE BENNETT

Snowshed

DENVER

SKAGWAY
shops and yard

TUNNEL
MOUNTAIN

Snowshed

Steel bridge

DEAD HORSE
GULCH

Covered turntable

Double-faced backdrop
extending well above eye level

LOG CABIN

16" radius

Multiply figured dimen-
sions and elevations by:
½″ for N
¾″ for TT
1″ for HO
1½″ for S
2″ for O
Crossing angle is the
same in all scales.

Ruled lines across plan are:
6″ apart in N
9″ apart in TT
12″ apart in HO
18″ apart in S
24″ apart in O
See page 70 for more data.

.ASER

Permanent snow fence

SKAGWAY
(downtown station)

WHITE PASS

Stations and Customs office

ALASKA TERRITORY
BRITISH COLUMBIA

Snowshed open on this side

101. White Pass & Yukon Ry. By John Armstrong. Conventional curves

The real WP&Y connects with steamers at each end and has no rail connections. It's a narrow-gauge line, but you can build it either narrow or standard as the curves are not too sharp. This is probably the most popular of all the fine layouts Armstrong has done.

Backdrop disappears into mountain

LYNN CANAL

SKAGWAY WHARF

⅛″ scale

⅔″ scale

PLAN INDEX

Arrangement: Plans are listed in same order as in the main part of this book. They are in order of size, but with a number of exceptions.

Plan size: is to the nearest foot in each scale.

Curve radii: are for curves limiting mainline operations.

Turnout size: Most plans use No. 4 or No. 6 track switches and exceptions are marked on the plan. If you don't care to build stub or custom switches, which usually aren't ready-made, you can often substitute No. 4 turnouts without any major changes.

Grades: are shown to nearest half per cent. These are a general guide as to how heavy a locomotive is needed to pull a given train. Grades are deliberately made stiffer than need be on some plans for visual effect.

Space shape: "Table" means two or more sides must be accessible for maintenance. "Front aisle" means other sides may be against walls. "Central aisle" reaches into space from outside; no ducking. "Open center" must be reached by ducking or via stairway. "Shelf" is narrow and usually can be bent around corners. See plan 94 for explanation of "radial aisle."

Operating pattern: "Oval" means any continuous route where track is not redoubled. Includes figure-eights, etc. "Return" means a loop or track which reverses direction of train one-way around oval. "Returns" allow reversal both ways. "Point" is a stub terminal. "Loop" is a return loop with or without a stub yard in conjunction with it. "Combination routing" is a particularly flexible arrangement consisting of a terminal-to-loop route using most if not all the main line available. In addition there are connecting tracks for oval running and returning in each direction around the oval. On some larger plans exact descriptions can't be made in the space of this index.

FOR N SCALE RAILROADS, DIVIDE THE HO DIMENSIONS BY 2

Plan No.	Width and length in feet				Minimum mainline radius in inches				Turnout frog No.	Mainline grade per cent	Plan No.	Name, space, operating scheme.
	TT	HO	S	O	TT	HO	S	O				
1	2x3	3x4	4x6	6x8	11¼	15	22½	30	4	4½	1	Stockton & Darlington RR. Table. Two-lap oval. Small yard.
2	3x3	3x4	5x6	7x7	11¼	15	22½	30	4	4½	2	Kettle Hills & Eastern RR. Table. Two-lap oval.
3	3x3	4x5	6x7	8x10	13½	18	27	36	4		3	Bay State Western Ry. Table. Double-track oval.
4	3x4	4x6	6x9	8x12	13½	18	27	36	4		4	Reddy River & Piedras RR. Table. Oval with roundhouse.
5	20x29	26x38	39x57	52x76	18	24	36	48	6		5	Atlantic Air Line. U-shelf. Loop to loop. Easy grades along shoreline.
6	1x5	1x6	2x9	3x12	13½	18	27	36	4		6	Switchman's Nightmare. Shelf. Yard only.
7	1x3	1x4	2x6	2x8	18	24	36	48	6		7	Apple Creek Junction Ry. Shelf. Yard only.
8	1x12	1x16	2x24	2x32	13½	18	27	36	4	4	8	Port Ogden & Northern RR. Shelf. Yards and switchback.
9	14x29	19x39	29x58	38x77	22½	30	45	60	6	2½	9	Erie RR. Shelf and central aisle. Complete system. Large yard.
10	2x5	3x6	5x9	6x12	11¼	15	22½	30	4		10	Pittsburgh, Midvale & Ironton RR. Table. Yard to industry.
11	3x4	4x5	5x8	7x10	18	24	36	48	6		11	Logan Square Yard. Corner shelf. Yard.
12	2x6	2x8	3x12	4x16	18	24	36	48	6		12	Mechanic Street Yard. Shelf. Yard.
13	3x5	3x7	5x10	6x14	13½	18	27	36	4		13	Elizabeth & Rahway Valley Ry. Table or front aisle. Oval with return.
14	3x5	4x7	6x10	8x13	13½	18	27	36	4	4	14	Blue Valley RR. Table or front aisle. Oval.
15	3x4	5x5	7x8	9x10	13½	18	27	36	4	4	15	Lake District Ry. Table. Three-lap oval.
16	3x5	4x6	5x9	7x13	11¼	15	22½	30	4		16	Valley Central Lines. Table. Oval.
17	3x5	4x7	5x10	7x13	11¼	15	22½	30	4	4½	17	Gorre & Daphetid RR. Front aisle or table. Two-lap oval and branch.
18	3x5	4x7	6x10	8x13	13½	18	27	36	4		18	Turtle River Industrial District. Front aisle or table. Oval.
19	3x5	4x6	5x9	7x13	13½	18	27	36	4		19	Dwight & Pontiac RR. Table. Oval. Shelf extension is extra width.
20	3x5	4x7	6x11	8x14	13½	18	27	36	4		20	New Industry Connecting RR. Table. Oval. Switching featured.
21	3x4	4x5	6x8	8x10	13½	18	27	36	4		21	Rockport & Oyster Bay Ry. Front aisle. Oval.
22	3x4	4x6	6x9	8x12	13½	18	27	36	4	3½	22	Tonopah & Salt Range RR. Table. Two-lap oval.
23	3x4	4x5	6x7	8x10	13½	18	27	36	4		23	Columbia & Cascade RR. Table. Oval.
24	3x6	4x8	6x12	8x16	13½	18	27	36	4	4	24	Toronto, Hamilton & Detroit RR. Table. Combination routing.
25	3x6	4x8	6x12	8x16	13½	18	27	36	4		25	Mohawk Southern Ry. Table. Oval.
26	3x6	4x8	6x12	8x16	13½	18	27	36	4		26	Pennsylvania & Potomac RR. Table. Oval and point to point.
27	3x6	4x8	6x12	8x16	13½	18	27	36	4	3½	27	Tremont & Cambridge RR. Table. Oval and terminal to loop.
28	3x6	4x8	6x12	8x16	13½	18	27	36	4	3½	28	Rock Island & Moline Belt Line. Table. Loop to loop and oval.
29	3x6	4x8	6x12	8x16	13½	18	27	36	4	4	29	Nantahala & Smoky Mountain Gorge RR. Front aisle or table. Two-lap oval.
30	3x6	4x8	6x12	8x16	11¼	15	22½	30	4	5½	30	Lime Ridge, Hercules & Portland RR. Table. Two-lap oval.

FOR N SCALE RAILROADS, DIVIDE THE HO DIMENSIONS BY 2

Plan No.	Width and length in feet				Minimum mainline radius in inches				Turnout frog No.	Mainline grade per cent	Plan No.	Name, space, operating scheme.
	TT	HO	S	O	TT	HO	S	O				
31	3x6	4x8	6x12	8x16	11¼	15	22½	30	4		31	Jersey Valley Central RR. Table or shelf. Two-lap oval.
32	3x6	4x8	6x12	8x16	11¼	15	22½	30	4		32	Custer & Front Range RR. Table. Oval.
33	3x6	4x8	6x12	8x16	11¼	15	22½	30	4	4	33	Bayside & Southampton Ry. Front aisle. Two-lap oval.
34	3x6	4x8	6x12	8x16	11¼	15	22½	30	Stub	4½	34	Laguna Plata RR. Front aisle. Point to point and oval.
35	3x6	4x8	6x12	8x16	9¾	13	19½	26	Stub	5½	35	Denver & South Park RR. Table. Oval with returns.
36	3x6	4x8	6x12	8x16	13½	18	27	36	4		36	Ft. Dodge & Elk City RR. Table. Oval. Depressed feature.
37	3x6	5x9	7x11	11x15	12	16	24	32	4	3½	37	Yankee Midland Ry. Table. Oval.
38	4x3	6x6	8x9	11x12	13½	18	27	36	4	3½	38	Central Missouri RR. Two-lap oval.
39	4x8	5x10	8x15	10x20	18	24	36	48	6		39	Denver & Northwestern RR. Table. Oval.
40	5x8	6x10	9x15	12x20	18	24	36	48	6	2	40	Troy & Mohawk Valley Ry. Open center. Loop to loop.
41	5x7	6x9	9x14	12x18	13½	18	27	36	4		41	Quaker State Eastern RR. Open center. Oval with alternate route.
42	5x5	6x7	8x11	11x14	13½	18	27	36	4	3½	42	Sanaxis & Phrax RR. Open center. Two-lap oval and return.
43	5x6	6x8	8x12	11x16	13½	18	27	36	4	3½	43	Deadwood, Big Horn & Pacific RR. Table. Loop to loop. Mining.
44	3x6	5x7	7x11	9x14	13½	18	27	36	4	4	44	Rockport & South Fork Lumber Co. Table. Point to point. Lumber. Grade optional.
45	6x8	8x10	12x15	16x20	13½	18	27	36	6	4	45	Superior & Iron Range RR. Central aisle. Point to point. Ore.
46	6x9	8x12	12x18	16x24	18	24	36	48	6	3	46	Jordan Valley RR. Central aisle. Ovals.
47	4x9	5x12	8x18	10x24	13½	18	27	36	4	3½	47	Cerro Azul RR. Table. Switchback. Elaborate yard.
48	7x9	9x12	14x18	18x24	18	24	36	48	6	3½	48	Virginia & Truckee RR. Central aisle. Point to point and oval. Old time.
49	6x8	9x11	13x16	17x21	18	24	36	48	Custom		49	Fairhaven & Ideal River RR. Display table. Oval with branch.
50	5x9	7x12	11x18	14x23	13½	18	27	36	4	4	50	Union & Overland RR. Open center. Point to loop and oval. Sectional frame.
51	6x9	8x12	11x18	15x23	13½	18	27	36	4		51	Chicago Inner Belt Line. L-shelf. Yards and industries.
52	6x6	8x8	12x12	16x16	18	24	36	48	6	2	52	Wisconsin Central RR. Open center. Two-lap oval and branch.
53	7x9	9x12	14x18	18x24	13½	18	27	36	4	3	53	New York, Ontario & Western RR. Open center. Oval with branch from wye to loop.
54	5x8	6x11	9x17	12x22	18	24	36	48	6	3	54	San Marino & Echo Mountain Ry. Front aisle and open center. Combination routing.
55	7x8	9x11	14x16	18x21	13½	18	27	36	Stub		55	Belfast & Moosehead Lake RR. U-shelf. Point to point.
56	5x9	6x12	9x18	12x24	22½	30	45	60	6		56	Dayton & Northern RR. Open center. Oval.
57	5x8	7x10	11x15	14x20	18	24	36	48	6	2½	57	Baltimore & Hudson RR. Front aisle and open center. Oval with returns. Popular.
58	7x9	10x13	15x17	20x26	18	24	36	48	6	2½	58	Grand River Western RR. Enlarged version of plan 57.
59	8x9	10x12	15x18	20x24	18	24	36	48	6	3	59	Great North Pass RR. Front aisle. Combination routing.
60	3x8	5x11	7x17	9x22	13½	18	27	36	6	2	60	Platonica River Southern RR. Table. Oval. Large yard.
61	5x11	7x15	11x23	14x30	13½	18	27	36	6	4	61	Dan Patch Lines. Enlarged version of plan 50.
62	9x9	12x12	18x18	24x24	18	24	36	48	6	2	62	Adirondack RR. Central aisle. Loop to loop, oval, and branch. Yard.
63	8x11	11x14	17x21	22x28	13½	18	27	36	Stub	4	63	Rio Grande Southern Ry. Central aisle. Point to point and oval.
64	8x11	10x15	15x23	20x30	18	24	36	48	6	3	64	Uniontown Southern RR. Open center. Oval with return.
65	7x11	9x14	14x21	18x28	18	24	36	48	6	3	65	Southern Cross Ry. Co. L-shaped. Oval with returns and branch. Yard.
66	7x11	9x14	14x21	19x28	21	28	42	56	6	3	66	Eureka, Shasta & Great Eastern Ry. L-shaped. Point to loop and oval.
67	7x10	10x14	14x20	19x27	13½	18	27	36	4	3½	67	Monon Route. Central aisle. Oval and returns.
68	9x12	12x16	18x24	24x32	18	24	36	48	4		68	Iron Ridge & Mayville RR. U-shelf. Point to point.

½" scale

1" scale

FOR N SCALE RAILROADS, DIVIDE THE HO DIMENSIONS BY 2

Plan No.	Width and length in feet				Minimum mainline radius in inches				Turncut frog No.	Mainline grade per cent	Plan No.	Name, space, operating scheme.
	TT	HO	S	O	TT	HO	S	O				
69	11x16	14x21	21x31	28x42	5½	7½	11	15	Custom		69	Union Bay Transit. Central aisle. Trolley routes. 7 per cent grade on branch.
70	4x7	5x9	8x14	10x18	9	12	18	24	Custom	5½	70	Springfield Electric Lines. Table. Trolley routes.
71	4x7	5x9	8x14	10x18	6¾	9	13½	18	Custom		71	Hillsboro Traction Co. Table. Trolley oval.
72	3x14	4x18	6x27	8x36	6¾	9	13½	18	Custom		72	Charles City Western RR. Shelf. Point to point and oval trolley.
73	8x15	10x20	15x30	20x40	13½	18	27	36	4	4	73	Golden Key Route. Open center. Suburban electric routes. Steam shuttle.
74	5x12	6x16	9x23	12x31	18	24	36	48	6	2½	74	Nickel Plate System. Open center. Two-lap oval. Large yard.
75	4x11	5x15	8x23	11x30	18	24	36	48	6	3	75	Thunderhead & Climax RR. Shelf. Switchback.
76	5x8	7x11	11x16	14x21	18	24	36	48	6	3	76	Ouachita & Ozark RR. Open center with shelf extension. Two-lap oval.
77	4x14	5x18	8x27	11x36	18	24	36	48	6	2	77	Jamaica & Kingsway Short Line. Table. Combination routing.
78	2x9	3x12	5x18	6x24	13½	18	27	36	4	5	78	Whitestone Cliffs Ry. Shelf. Switchback from quarry to wharf.
79	6x14	9x19	13x28	17x38	22½	30	45	60	6	2	79	Frisco Lines. Open center. Two-lap oval. Large yard.
80	5x11	7x15	10x22	13x30	18	24	36	48	6	3½	80	East Bay Belt Line. Front aisle and open center. Ovals and returns.
81	3x15	4x20	6x30	8x40	13½	18	27	36	6		81	San Diego & Arizona Eastern RR. Shelf. Terminal to loop.
82	7x15	9x21	14x31	18x41	18	24	36	48	6		82	Toledo & Southern Michigan RR. Front aisle and open center. Loop to loop plus branch. Easy grades.
83	8x13	10x18	15x26	20x36	13½	18	27	36	4	2½	83	Yosemite Valley RR. Central aisle. Point to point. Could be one-level.
84	8x15	10x20	15x30	20x40	22½	30	45	60	6	2	84	The Wiscona Route. Open center. Combination routing.
85	8x14	10x19	15x28	20x37	22½	30	45	60	6	2	85	Ardmore, Cadosia & Fairmill RR. Variation of plan 84.
86	8x15	10x20	15x30	20x40	18	24	36	48	Mixed	3	86	Cajon Pass, Salt Lake & Santa Fe RR. Open center. Loop to loop and oval.
87	8x14	10x18	15x27	20x36	13½	18	27	36	4	4	87	Pacific Great Eastern RR. Table. Point to point. Could be one-level.
88	11x15	15x20	23x30	30x40	18	24	36	48	4, 6	3	88	Chesapeake & Ohio RR. Front and central aisle. Point to point and oval.
89	10x15	14x20	20x30	37x39	18	24	36	48	6		89	Bednigo & Pine River RR. Open center. Terminal to loop and oval.
90	9x15	12x21	18x31	24x41	22½	30	45	60	6	2	90	Atlanta, Birmingham & Columbus RR. L-shaped. Combination routing.
91	11x12	15x16	23x25	30x33	27	36	54	72	6		91	Toledo & Indiana RR. Display case. Oval. Central workshop.
92	9x14	12x19	18x29	25x38	18	24	36	48	6	2	92	Missouri-Kansas-Texas System. Open center. Ovals and returns. Trolley branch.
93	11x17	14x23	21x35	28x46	22½	30	45	60	6	2	93	Tennessee Eastern Ry. T-table. Oval with return. Wye and terminal.
94	40x45	53x60	80x90	106x120	27	36	54	72	8	1½	94	Eureka & Golden Gate RR. Radial aisle. Loop to loop. Idea plan.
95	11x28	14x38	21x57	28x76	13½	18	27	36	4	4	95	Hungry Horse Timber Co. Radial aisle. Point to point with loops.
96	2x15	3x20	5x30	6x40	12	16	24	32	6	4	96	Orrville Mining RR. Shelf. Switchback.
97	9x20	12x26	18x39	24x52	22½	30	45	60	6	3	97	Philadelphia & Reading System. Table. Combination routing. Complex.
98	11x13	14x17	21x25	28x34	18	24	36	48	6	2	98	Butte, Anaconda & Pacific RR. Central aisles. Point to point and oval.
99	35x40	47x53	70x80	94x106	Various broad radii.				6	2	99	South Bend, South Shore & Chicago RR. Central aisle table. Complete railroad.
100	12x14	16x19	24x29	32x38	18	24	36	48	6	2	100	Ohio Central Lines. L-shaped. Combination routing.
101	15x15	20x20	30x30	40x40	18	24	36	48	6	4	101	White Pass & Yukon Ry. Central aisle. Point to point.